FREEMASONRY

JACK *HARRIS*

ш
WHITAKER
HOUSE

Unless otherwise indicated, all Scripture quotations are taken from the King James Version (KJV) of the Bible.

Scripture quotations marked (NKJV) are taken from the *New King James Version,* © 1979, 1980, 1982 by Thomas Nelson, Inc. Used by permission. All rights reserved.

Editorial note: Even at the cost of violating grammatical rules, we have chosen not to capitalize the name satan and related names.

FREEMASONRY

ISBN: 0-88368-669-4
Printed in the United States of America
© 1983 by Jack Harris

Whitaker House
30 Hunt Valley Circle
New Kensington, PA 15068

Library of Congress Cataloging-in-Publication Data

Harris, Jack, 1936–
  Freemasonry / by Jack Harris.
    p. cm.
Includes bibliographical references.
  ISBN 0-88368-669-4
  1. Freemasonry—Rituals. 2. Freemasonry–Religious
aspects–Christianity. I. Title.
  HS459 .H32 2001
  366'.1—dc21   2001001978

1 2 3 4 5 6 7 8 9 10 11 12 13 / 08 07 06 05 04 03 02 01

Contents

Foreword

Freemasonry is a straightforward exposé of the Ancient, Free, and Accepted Masons, more popularly known as Freemasonry. Mr. Jack Harris, the author of this interesting book, is an expert witness to the teachings and practices of this worldwide organization. For a number of years he was a Master Mason, rising to the position of Worshipful Master, the highest elected office in Blue Lodge Masonry. He also passed through all the degrees of the York Rite, the so-called "Christian" branch of Freemasonry. Mr. Harris, therefore, speaks on the subject of Freemasonry "as one having authority."

The author concisely explains to the reader the basic doctrines and goals of the Freemasons, showing how they deviate from biblical Christianity. All the secret passwords, oaths, obligations, and grips of Masonry are herein revealed, including the "supreme Masonic word," known only to Master Masons.

If you have ever been curious about the origin and beliefs of Freemasonry, *Freemasonry* is the book for you.

—Rev. R. Alan Streett, Ph.D.

Preface

❦

This book basically deals with Blue Lodge Masonry (first, second, and third degrees), its roots, and interpretations of rituals. Only the very basic essentials of the Blue Lodge degrees are covered; by no means is this book meant to be an exhaustive study into the cult of Freemasonry. Scottish Rite and York Rite Masonry are only briefly mentioned, because these degrees rise or fall on the first three degrees of Blue Lodge. If, as evidence supports the foundational (Blue Lodge) degrees are satanic, it stands to reason that the York and Scottish Rite degrees, along with branches for women and children, are as well.

The only pure forms of Freemasonry are the Blue Lodge with the Royal Arch degree. All other degrees are "add-on" degrees, and are not, as such, a part of the original plan of Masonry. Supreme power and authority over all Masons originates in the various Blue Lodges. I will use the Word of God to expose this anti-Christian cult and its damnable heresies—teachings (or doctrines) that have been heaped upon the body of Christ (the church) for thousands of years.

I believe the humanistic teachings of Freemasonry in all of its branches will be a primary catalyst allowing the antichrist and one-world apostate church to come to power during the Tribulation period. The spiritual welfare of the church and the sanctification of believers are the primary concerns of this book.

A ministry that sets forth Freemasonry as a cult may appear to be both unusual and, for some, very distasteful. But it is important to understand the God-given motivation for writing this book. Its purpose is to allow God to speak through His revelation, the Bible, in order to convince all readers of the satanic nature of a cult unchecked for many years—even to the point of penetrating our pulpits and teaching ministries. I believe the Spirit of God has guided the writing of this book.

A cult is defined as any group that embraces, teaches, or practices religious doctrine contrary to the accepted and established truth of biblical Christianity.

The term *Freemasonry* encompasses every group under the direct influence of Freemasonry, whether originated or controlled by the Freemasons. Such groups include (and this list is by no means exhaustive): Blue Lodge of the three degrees, Scottish Rite, York Rite, Job's Daughters, Rainbow Girls, Tall Cedars, DeMolay, Daughters of the Nile, Ancient Arabic Order Nobles Mystic Shrine (A.A.O.N.M.S.), and Square clubs. To detail the complete fundamentals of this cult and its branches would encompass many volumes and would go beyond the scope of this book. The information given here should be sufficient to prove the heretical nature of the beliefs and practices of the Freemasons.

Many objections may arise to this type of book, especially from Christians committed through initiation to Freemasonry. However, if a person is truly sincere in seeking the truth, he will find it in the words of Jesus who said, *"I am the way, the truth, and the life: no man cometh unto the Father, but by me"* (John 14:6).

God's Word clearly states that truth frees man from the penalty and power of sin. This freedom is contingent upon a personal relationship with Jesus Christ as Savior. The Bible proclaims man a sinner. He is forgiven through Christ's death on the cross and resurrection from the dead, *"that whosoever believeth in him should not perish, but have everlasting life"* (John 3:16).

Personal Testimony

In 1961, prior to my accepting Jesus Christ as my personal Savior, I was approached very subtly and asked, "What do you think about Freemasonry?" My answer demonstrated ignorance on the subject. I mentioned that I believed that only morally good people and devout Christians belonged to the lodge (an opinion and false concept shared by a large segment of the church today). I was then indirectly asked to consider joining the Freemasons. The reasons for my deciding to seek membership were based on the mystery, intrigue, and secrecy involved, as well as the fact that many in my church, along with the minister, were members of the Freemasons.

Three lodge members visited me to investigate my character. A friendly conversation evolved, including the following questions:

"Were you ever convicted of a crime?"

"What church do you attend?"

"What are your interests?"

"Are you married or divorced?"

The vote and acceptance for my initiation into the first three degrees of Freemasonry occurred in May 1961. Six months later, I was asked to become an officer of the lodge.

In 1963, I was petitioned and accepted into the Royal Arch chapter of Masons, Royal and Select Masters or Council, and Knights Templar or Commandery. Shortly thereafter, I joined the Shrine (A.A.O.N.M.S.). Following seven years of progression from one office to another, called *chairs*, I was installed as Worshipful Master of the lodge. This was done only after completing exhaustive memory work and being examined and elected. My installation as Worshipful Master of a Baltimore lodge took place in January 1968.

During the process of moving through the various chairs (from office to office), God opened my eyes to the deceptions of Freemasonry. An awareness of my own spiritual condition resulted.

One evening following a meeting, the Chaplain closed his prayers with the phrase, "in the name of the Lord Jesus Christ." An objection was given to this closing. Usually a universal quotation from the *Masonic Manual* (blue book) is given at the beginning and end of all prayers. I was shocked by this objection. I always thought that wherever God is worshipped and reverenced, even in the lodge room, a prayer should never exclude His Son, Jesus Christ.

A second indication of deception surfaced during the year I was installed as Worshipful Master. By appointment, I visited the Grand Lodge of Maryland and requested a Christian flag be placed next to my chair in the lodge room. The Grand Master refused on the grounds that such a flag would offend our Jewish, Moslem, and Hindu members. This incident was very upsetting. My faith in Masonry was fading.

Two years later, in October 1970, God's conviction was heavy upon me as a sinner. I repented and asked Jesus to forgive me for having rejected Him. That night in my living room I accepted Jesus Christ as my Savior. This experience, combined with intense Bible study for the next two years, convinced me to renounce Freemasonry and all its branches in May 1972.

God has since opened many doors of opportunity to witness in churches, on the radio, and in a seminary, impressing upon believers the dangers of Freemasonry. The foundational doctrines of the Christian faith contrast with Freemasonry and its associated teachings, all of which are based upon ancient pagan and satanic rituals. Is it any wonder that some of Christendom's spiritual giants such as Moody, Finney, Torrey, Barnhouse, and Rice have vigorously opposed Freemasonry?

My goal is to inform all Christians of the danger of committing themselves by oath to this satanic cult. "Once a Mason, always a Mason" is the intended result when one obligates himself to Masonry. However, it is important to consider God's Word, which says, *"If the Son therefore shall make you free, ye shall be free indeed"* (John 8:36).

Freemasonry is one of satan's master deceptions. Many ministers, elders, deacons, trustees, and Sunday school teachers belong to this cult. There is a tremendous need to scrutinize the cultic nature of Freemasonry in view of its infiltration into the church and the negative effects that result. It should be exposed to the true light of God's redeeming Word.

The structure of this book is intended to model the book of John. The apostle John presented the person of Jesus Christ within the framework of a typical courtroom scene. The defense pursued the case to rightly identify the deity of Christ. Freemasonry will be presented in the same way: what Freemasonry says about itself, what others say about it, and what Freemasonry actually does in its rituals. The verdict stands pronounced in the conclusion.

One

Spiritual Temples

God's Word is very explicit as to what constitutes a true spiritual temple. We must assume that any spiritual temple being built must be tested and judged as to its validity. God calls the body of believers temples of the Holy Spirit. Also, believers are fitted together with the prophets and apostles to form a holy spiritual building, called the church. Jesus Christ is the Chief Cornerstone of this spiritual building.

Freemasonry teaches that the body of an initiated Mason is a temple, and together, Masons worldwide form the larger corporate temple of Freemasonry.

The following verses give an overview of the Scripture's position regarding spiritual temples:

> Ye also, as living stones, are built up a spiritual house, an holy priesthood, to offer up spiritual sacrifices acceptable to God through Jesus Christ. Therefore it is also contained in the Scripture, "Behold, I lay in Zion a chief cornerstone, elect, precious, and he who believes on Him will by no means be put to shame."
>
> (1 Peter 2:5–6 NKJV)

For we are labourers together with God: ye are God's husbandry, ye are God's building. According to the grace of God which is given unto me, as a wise master-builder, I have laid the foundation, and another buildeth thereon. But let every man take heed how he buildeth thereupon. For other foundation can no man lay than that is laid, which is Jesus Christ. Now if any man build upon this foundation gold, silver, precious stones, wood, hay, stubble; every man's work shall be made manifest: for the day shall declare it, because it shall be revealed by fire; and the fire shall try every man's work of what sort it is. If any man's work abide which he hath built thereupon, he shall receive a reward. If any man's work shall be burned, he shall suffer loss: but he himself shall be saved; yet so as by fire. Know ye not that ye are the temple of God, and that the Spirit of God dwelleth in you? If any man defile the temple of God, him shall God destroy; for the temple of God is holy, which temple ye are. Let no man deceive himself. If any man among you seemeth to be wise in this world, let him become a fool, that he may be wise. For the wisdom of this world is foolishness with God. For it is written, He taketh the wise in their own craftiness. And again, The Lord knoweth the thoughts of the wise, that they are vain. Therefore let no man glory in men. For all things are yours; whether Paul, or Apollos, or Cephas, or the world, or life, or death, or things present, or things to come; all are yours; and ye are Christ's; and Christ is God's. (1 Corinthians 3:9–23)

And are built upon the foundation of the apostles and prophets, Jesus Christ himself being the chief corner stone. (Ephesians 2:20)

God is building spiritual temples through the finished work of Christ, the Chief Cornerstone: The power to build these temples comes from the Holy Spirit. Any attempt to construct a spiritual temple using any other cornerstone is not biblical. It is a satanic counterfeit. (See 1 Corinthians 2:12-16; Ephesians 3:16-19; John 16:13-14.) Such activity is being manifested today through various cults.

Satan uses individuals and groups as agents in the building of false temples. Carefully read the following verses:

> For if he that cometh preacheth another Jesus, whom we have not preached, or if ye receive another spirit, which ye have not received, or another gospel, which ye have not accepted, ye might well bear with him.
> (2 Corinthians 11:4)

> And no marvel; for Satan himself is transformed into an angel of light. Therefore, it is no great thing if his ministers also be transformed as the ministers of righteousness, whose end shall be according to their works.
> (2 Corinthians 11:14-15)

In Galatians 1:6-10, Paul pronounced a divine curse on all who would preach any other gospel except that which Christ had given him. No one preaching false doctrine was excluded from the curse. Two separate spiritual forces are at work in the world. One is of God; the other is of satan. Which one of these two spiritual forces controls Freemasonry?

Since Freemasonry builds upon a false foundation, which is in opposition to God's Word, its source or origin must be demonic.

Albert Mackey, in his book *Encyclopedia of Freemasonry*, referred to the great Masonic doctrine of a spiritual temple:

> We erect temples for virtue and dungeons for vice....There is no symbolism of the order more sublime than that in which the Speculative Mason is supposed to be engaged...the construction of a spiritual temple, alluding to that material temple which was erected by his operative predecessors at Jerusalem.
>
> The difference in this point of view, between operative and speculative Masonry, is simply this, that while the former was engaged on Mt. Moriah of a material temple of stones and cedar, gold and precious stones, the latter is occupied from his first initiation to his last in the construction, adornment and completion of the spiritual temple of his body.

Albert Mackey is considered the greatest of all Masonic authors; his statement encompasses all that Freemasonry tries to accomplish in degree work.

The headquarters of the Scottish Rite Masonry, S.J. (Southern Jurisdiction), is located at 1733 Sixteenth Street, N.W., Washington, D.C. Engraved in stone over the entrance is the following statement: "Freemasonry builds temples in the hearts of men and nations."

Freemasonry teaches spiritual doctrine and admonishes practices that are supposed to relate to one's moral life. Its teachings are not of God. *Webster's Dictionary* defines *spiritual* as "that which pertains to religion, that which is sacred and applies to the soul and spirit." Freemasonry enters this realm of life, but it enters not by way of the Savior, Jesus Christ. It enters instead by the back door of good deeds, community service, and secret rite.

Masonry is indeed in the business of building spiritual temples in the hearts of initiates. We will examine carefully the process for establishing these temples.

First, the lodge room is constructed in such a way as to resemble the basic floor plan of King Solomon's temple. The following is a quote from the Masonic ritual, as found in the *Maryland Masonic Manual*.

> Lodges are situated due east and west because King Solomon's temple was so situated. King Solomon's temple was so situated because, when Moses had safely conducted the children of Israel through the Red Sea, when pursued by Pharaoh and his hosts, he there, by divine command, erected a tabernacle, in commemoration of that mighty east wind by which their miraculous deliverance was wrought. This tabernacle was situated due east and west, and was an exact model of King Solomon's temple, of which all Lodges are, or should be, representations.

Various tools indicate the degrees of Masonry and are symbols teaching the candidate how to conduct his life, and thereby building the temple of his soul according to Masonic beliefs. We will examine a few of the tools of the first three degrees of Masonry, as taken directly from the *Maryland Masonic Manual*.

The Gavel—First Degree

The Common Gavel is an instrument made use of by operative Masons to break off the corners of rough stones, the better to fit them for the builder's use; but we, as Free and Accepted Masons, are taught to make use of it for the more noble and glorious purpose of divesting our hearts and consciences of all the vices and superfluities of life; thereby fitting our minds as living stones for that spiritual building, that house *"not made with hands, eternal in the heavens"* (2 Corinthians 5:1).

The Plumb, Square, and Level—Second Degree

The Plumb admonishes us to walk uprightly in our several stations before God and man, squaring our actions by the square of virtue, and remembering that we are traveling upon the level of time, to "that undiscovered country from whose bourne no traveler returns."

The Trowel—Third Degree

The Working Tools of a Master Mason are all the implements of Masonry indiscriminately, but more especially the Trowel. The Trowel is an instrument made use of by operative Masons, to spread the cement which unites a building into one common mass; but we as Free and Accepted Masons are taught to make use of it for the more noble and glorious purpose of spreading the cement

of brotherly love and affection; that cement
unites us into one sacred band, or society of frien
and brothers, among whom no contention should
ever exist, but that noble contention, or rather emu-
lation, of who can best work and best agree.

These are just a few of the working tools of Masonry
that are used by Masons to build their spiritual temples.
None of these tools is biblical and therefore cannot be
used to build a true spiritual temple. According to the
Masons' own explanation of the tools, they are using
human effort alone to attain spiritual perfection, thus
deifying man and promising him heaven on earth. In
other words, character and good deeds determine the
destiny of the Mason, not the finished work of Jesus
Christ. In contradistinction, Galatians 2:20–21 states,

> I am crucified with Christ: nevertheless, I live; yet not I,
> but Christ liveth in me: and the life which I now live in
> the flesh I live by the faith of the Son of God, who loved
> me, and gave himself for me. I do not frustrate [make
> void] the grace of God: for if righteousness come by the
> law, then Christ is dead in vain.

It is important here to briefly analyze the tabernacle
in the wilderness built by Moses for the worship of
Jehovah God. King Solomon's temple was built according to the same basic design and for the same purpose.
As the priest approaches the brazen altar, he is reminded
of the sheep and oxen slain for the blood sacrifices to
God. These sacrifices were symbols of Jesus Christ, the
Lamb of God sacrificed for our sins upon the cross (John
1:29).

From this point the priest proceeds to the laver to wash his hands before entering the Holy Place. This reminds him that the blood cleanses from all sin (1 John 1:7). As the high priest enters the Holy Place he sees the showbread on his right and the candlesticks on his left. The Word of God reveals to us that Jesus Christ is the Light of the World (John 8:12) and the Bread of Life (John 6:35), which these pieces of furniture represented.

Just before the high priest entered the Holy of Holies, he would see the altar of incense, which is symbolic of the prayer of Christ in John 17. This altar of incense is before the throne of God in heaven. In the Holy of Holies is the ark of the covenant, with the mercy seat resting upon the top as a lid. It was upon this mercy seat that the blood of the lamb was sprinkled for the forgiveness of the sins of the children of Israel. The Bible tells us that Christ is now our Mercy Seat (1 John 2:2; Hebrews 7:27).

If we were to draw a line from the brazen altar to the ark of the covenant, and then draw an intersecting line perpendicular from the candlesticks to the showbread, we would have a cross. The tabernacle in the wilderness and the temple of Solomon were meant to point to Jesus Christ. When Christ came in the flesh and sacrificed Himself on the cross for us, He said, *"It is finished"* (John 19:30). This put an end to ceremonial sacrifices with animals. (See Hebrews 9:11–12.)

Not only are Masonic lodges erected east and west because King Solomon's temple was so situated, but

Masonic ritual is a mockery of the ceremonial ritual of Old Testament sacrifices.

Just as one example, in the second, or Fellowcraft, degree of Masonry, the Mason comes into the lodge's Holy of Holies by his own self-efforts. When he is introduced to the Worshipful Master, who represents King Solomon, he is given an explanation of the letter G situated above the Master's Chair in the East. This letter G signifies *geometry* and *deity*. Is this what the Bible tells us was in the Holy of Holies? The pagan god of Freemasonry represented by the letter G is not the God of the Bible, and so Masonry has desecrated the name of God by its pagan rituals.

We approach God through the finished work of Jesus Christ, not our ability to remember some rituals, due guards, grips, and words.

Two

Origins

❦

I n order to best understand a philosophy, religion, or cult, it is necessary to go back to its beginnings, to consider its origin—its *foundations and forefathers.*

There are two divisions of Freemasonry: operative and speculative. Operative Masonry refers to actual stonemasons who possessed the skills and art of stonecutting and setting, traceable back to the Tower of Babel. According to God's Word, the tower was not of God's design, but satan's handiwork. Tracing the art of stonemasonry, through time we come to the pyramids of Egypt, Mexico, and South America. Secular history confirms that the religion of the ancient stonemasons from Egypt and Babel was pagan worship. Carrying the operative art to the building and rebuilding of King Solomon's temple between 949 B.C. and 520 B.C., the skilled artisans for King Solomon's temple had to be taken from Phoenicia, a country now known as Lebanon. The religion of that country was Baal worship, originating from the Egyptians.

It is important to pause a minute at King Solomon's temple. It is upon this that Freemasonry, as it exists today, bases much of its degree work. King Solomon is Freemasonry's first most excellent Grand Master—but only symbolically, not actually.

Since King Solomon knew very little about cedar cutting or stonecutting, he made a covenant with Hiram, king of Tyre, in the country of Phoenicia, to hire stonemasons to build the temple. Hiram, king of Tyre, was half Jew and half Phoenician. This covenant, along with the marriage of King Solomon to Pharaoh's daughter, as recorded in 1 Kings, was the primary catalyst of King Solomon's rebellion against God and his turning to idol worship.

The ancient mysteries of Egypt, from which Masonry draws a great deal of its rituals, originated at the Tower of Babel. The Phoenician stonemasons (cedar cutters) of Tyre and Sidon were used to build the temple of Solomon, employing Jewish labor. Their pagan practices greatly influenced the Jews in Jerusalem during Solomon's reign and thereafter caused them to fall into idolatry, which was at its height during the reign of King Ahab. King Ahab allowed his wife, Jezebel, to bring in 450 priests of Baal from Egypt to practice pagan worship in Jerusalem. Thus, the stone builders of the Tower of Babel, the pyramids, and Solomon's temple were for the most part idol worshippers.

The conquests of the Roman Empire included nations whose people possessed such crafts and skills as stonecutting and setting, such as the Egyptians and Phoenicians. The great architecture of Rome flourished as a result. By the fourth century A.D., Constantine, emperor of Rome, would not allow any skilled craftsman to abandon his trade or leave his dwelling place. Sons were compelled to learn and practice their fathers' trades. Collectively called the Roman College of Artifices, these craftsmen were responsible for the transmission of stonecutting and setting skills through the ninth century to cathedral and castle builders throughout Europe. Practicing stonemasons met in lodges, sometimes called guilds, where they found fellowship with others of their craft.

The religion of most ninth-century stonemasons was Roman Catholic, and loyalty to the Catholic Church was a must. However, during the Reformation in England in 1517, the cathedral stonemasons were very inactive. From this time until 1717, operative stonemason guilds were practically extinct. With the Roman authority over trade unions gone, and cathedral building at a standstill, lodges were reduced to four in the south of England by 1717. However, the "gentlemen" Masons, or Freemasons, were increasing rapidly. These knew nothing about operative Masonry. Their growing number, money, and power rekindled the dying art of Masonic rite. With all but a few operative Masons left, the gentlemen Masons sought to revive festivals of the old guilds and formed the Institution of Speculative Masonry in 1717.

Rev. James Anderson and Rev. John T. Desaguiliers took the tools of the builders' trade and applied symbolic meanings to them for moral instruction in a Masonic life. At the same time, they disguised in biblical terminology the ancient pagan mysteries of Egypt and other rites used in the Masonic rituals.

Rev. James Anderson (1680–1739) was a Presbyterian minister in Swallow Falls, England. Scottish by descent, he was born in Edinborough and formulated with Desaguiliers the first three degrees of Freemasonry. Rev. John T. Desaguiliers (1683–1744) was a natural philosopher, inventor, and Protestant minister, and the son of a Protestant minister. He was born in France and later journeyed to England with his father in 1685 at the age of two.

Only the first three degrees of Freemasonry are "pure" Freemasonry, as is the Royal Arch degree. All other degrees, such as Scottish Rite, York Rite, and Shrine, are modern derivatives not tied to the origins of pure Freemasonry.

Albert Pike (1809–1891) and Albert G. Mackey (1807–1881) were considered the two best interpreters of all Masonic ritual. Albert Mackey, desiring to contribute to the elevation of the order, spent some thirty-five years interpreting the degrees of Freemasonry and produced a book entitled *Encyclopedia of Freemasonry*. Mackey, due to his long and intense study, became almost blind. He was Worshipful Master of Solomon Lodge in 1842, a doctor, and a thirty-three degree Mason. He held the highest offices of Freemasonry in the Scottish and York Rites.

Albert Pike was born in Boston, Massachusetts. He was a teacher and a brigadier general in the Civil War. Later, he was tried for treason. He held the highest office in Scottish Rite Masonry and rewrote all Scottish Rite rituals, which are still practiced today. These rituals are pagan and occultic in design. Mr. Pike was an admitted luciferian, believing that two coequal Gods exist in the universe: lucifer, the god of good and light, and Adonay, the Christian god, who rules evil and darkness.

The religious beliefs of Albert Pike should be considered as they are found in the instructions issued by him on July 4, 1889, to the twenty-three Supreme Councils of the world. That which we must say to the crowd is, "We worship a God, but it is the God that one adores without superstition." To you, Sovereign Grand Inspectors General, we say this, that you may repeat it to the Brethren of the thirty-second, thirty-first, and thirtieth degrees: "The Masonic religion should be, by all of us initiates of the high degrees, maintained in the purity of the Luciferian doctrine. If lucifer were not God, would Adonay (the God of the Christians) whose deeds prove his cruelty, perfidy, and hatred of man, barbarism, and repulsion for science—would Adonay and his priests calumniate him? Yes, lucifer is God and unfortunately Adonay is also God. For the eternal law is that there is no light without shade, no beauty without ugliness, no white without black, for the absolute can only exist as two Gods: darkness being necessary to light to serve as its foil, as the pedestal is necessary to the statue, and the brake to the locomotive. In analogical and universal dynamics one can only lean on that which will resist. Thus the universe is balanced by two forces which maintain its equilibrium: the force of attraction and that of repulsion. These two forces exist in physics, philosophy, and religion. And the scientific reality of the divine dualism is demonstrated by the phenomena of polarity and by the universal law of sympathies and antipathies. That is why the intelligent disciples of Zoroaster, as well as, after them, the Gnostics, the Manicheans, and the Templars, have admitted, as the only logical metaphysical conception, the system of the two divine principles fighting eternally, and one cannot believe the one inferior in power to the other. Thus, the doctrine of satanism is a heresy; and the true and pure philosophic religion is the belief in lucifer, the equal Adonay; but lucifer, god of light and god of good, is struggling for humanity against Adonay, the God of Darkness and Evil."

At the time of this declaration, Pike accepted simultaneously the positions of Grand Master of the Central Directory of Washington, Grand Commander of the Supreme Council of Charleston, and Sovereign Pontiff of Universal Freemasonry. He is looked upon today as the foremost literary genius of Masonry and is probably best known for his famous work *Morals and Dogma*.[1]

_____

[1]Lady Queensborough, *Occult Theocracy* (Christian Book Club of America, 1931).

Three

Branches of Freemasonry and Knights Templar

When a man submits his application to Masonry, it is only for the first degrees. All other degrees must be applied for separately. This can be done only after the third degree is reached. It is significant to note here that no woman can be made a Mason. This is stated both as a part of the third degree obligation and in the eighteenth landmark of Masonry. The Mason must be a man, freeborn, at least twenty-one years of age, and not physically impaired as to prevent him from making the various due guards, or movements, and signs with his hands and feet. These due guards and signs are part of the rituals of the first three degrees of Freemasonry.

The first three degrees are called "Entered Apprentice," "Fellowcraft," and "Master Mason." Each degree is received upon having passed the examination in the previous degree. After a candidate takes his first degree, he must attend a class to memorize the various aspects of the degree through which he has gone, including a variety of blood-curdling oaths. Everything is taught orally; nothing can be written down. One could spend two to three hours a night for two weeks memorizing all the pagan rituals for each degree. Examination is in open lodge with members and officers present. One must pass before he can proceed to the next degree.

If a member of Freemasonry does not pay his dues to the Blue Lodge, he loses his privileges to attend in good standing all other branches of Freemasonry. In the Blue Lodge, all candidates for membership must participate in the rituals. This is also true of York Rite Masonry.

Freemasonry is divided as follows:

- ❧ Blue Lodge, instituted as a speculative science in 1717.
- ❧ York Rite Freemasonry, consisting of Chapter of Royal Arch, founded in 1750; Council R.A.S.M. (Royal And Select Masters), the next step; and Commandery of Knights Templar, which originated in the United States in 1816.
- ❧ Scottish Rite, composed of thirty degrees, along with the first three degrees of Blue Lodge, which equal thirty-three degrees. It was built on the rite of perfection of twenty-five degrees and was devised in the College of Clermount in 1854. Albert Pike was the man responsible for revising the Scottish Rite while serving as Grand Commander from 1859 until 1891. It should be noted here

that the Scottish Rite is not only pagan, but is also the most demonic and occult branch of Freemasonry.

🌿 The Shrine (A.A.O.N.M.S.). A candidate must be a thirty-two-degree Mason or Knights Templar to apply. It is Muslim-oriented with a Muslim death oath.

🌿 Tall Cedars of Lebanon. All Master Masons are eligible.

🌿 De Molay, for boys from fourteen to twenty-one years of age.

🌿 Eastern Star, for women whose relatives are Masons.

🌿 Job's Daughters, for the daughters of Masons.

🌿 Rainbow Girls and Daughters of the Nile, also for the daughters of Masons.

🌿 Various Square clubs, which are organizations to which any Mason can belong.

None of these branches could or would exist without the basic Blue Lodge, the hub of all Freemasonry. All power and authority come from the Grand Lodges in the U.S.A., as well as the various Blue Lodges.

One branch of Freemasonry claims to be Christian. This is the Commandery of Knights Templar, which projects symbols like banners of crosses; celebrates such Christian holidays as Easter, Christmas, and Ascension Day; and parades in uniforms into the churches.

Prerequisites for membership into Knights Templar include passing all three degrees of the Blue Lodge and the Royal Arch degree. Then the individual must have taken approximately seven oaths or obligations, putting his hand on the Bible, kissing it after each oath. Each of these oaths include horrible penalties if the secrets of Masonry are revealed. The teachings, beliefs, and doctrines issued from these oaths are anti-Christian, mocking God in word and deed. It is upon this foundation that a Mason submits his application into a branch of Freemasonry that calls itself Christian.

The name of Knights Templar comes from the Crusaders. To use the Crusaders as an example of the Christian faith is similar to using communism as an example of freedom.

The Crusaders were the most disgraceful, degrading group of men ever to wear the symbol of the cross and pretend to defend Christian truth. It is a fact of history that the Crusaders fell into cultic and occultic practices and embraced heretical teachings shortly after their inception. These heretical practices were brought to a head when Pope Leo put Sir Knight Jock Du Molay to death at a burning stake on March 14, 1314, for heresy.[1] Fifty-four knights who were under Jock Du Molay were also burned at the stake in France, May 12, 1310. The Crusaders' name stayed buried until Freemasonry revived it and its practices five hundred years later, giving it a Christian flavor.

Two basic facts should be reemphasized here. The first is that Knights Templar originated in the Roman Catholic Church, under complete authority of the Pope. The Pope later ordered the leader burned at the stake and disgraced the rest as heretics. The second is that prerequisite for membership must be the first three degrees of Freemasonry.

Consider one of the oaths taken in the name of Christianity. In the degree of Knights Templar and Knights of Malta (one of the degrees of Knights Templar), the candidate is given an account of what he has passed. He takes a cup, which is the upper part of a skull, and repeats after the Grand Commander the following obligation:

> This pure wine I now take in testimony of my belief in the mortality of the body and the immortality of the soul, and may this libation appear as a witness against me both here and hereafter, and as the sins of the world were laid upon the head of the Savior, so may all the sins committed by the person whose skull this was be heaped upon my head in addition to my own, should I ever knowingly or willingly violate or transgress any obligation that I have heretofore taken, taken at this time, or shall at any future period take, in relation to any degree of Masonry or order of Knighthood. So help me God.

A horrible implication is here. These Knights Templar and Knights of Malta take oaths sustained by a horrid penalty, incurred not merely for violation of the particular obligation of this degree, but any obligation that has been taken heretofore, taken at this time, or taken at any future period in relation to any degree of Masonry or order of Knighthood.

This is called the sealed obligation. Here in the most solemn manner, the candidate, drinking wine out of a human skull, takes upon himself this obligation under the penalty of a double damnation. What can exceed the profanity and wickedness of this? Even though all of Freemasonry is cultic, and, in some instances, occultic, it is grievous to see such groups as Knights Templar make claims to be Christian when it has been proven that their rituals are a disgrace to the Savior.

Jehovah's Witnesses, Mormons, Christian Scientists, and other adherents to cults in this country claim to be Christian and use the Bible to back up their beliefs and practices. The fact that a group calls itself "Christian," requires certain "Christian" practices for membership, and uses biblical terminology does not mean it is a Christian organization.

God's Word is very clear on this subject. Matthew 12:33-37 says,

> Either make the tree good, and his fruit good; or else make the tree corrupt, and his fruit corrupt: for the tree is known by his fruit. O generation of vipers, how can ye, being evil, speak good things? For out of the abundance of the heart the mouth speaketh. A good man out of the good treasure of the heart bringeth forth good things: and an evil man out of the evil treasure bringeth forth evil things. But I say unto you, That every idle word that men shall speak, they shall give account of it in the day of judgment. For by thy words thou shalt be justified, and by thy words thou shalt be condemned.

Further clarification from God's Word to this subject comes from Matthew 7:15-20, which says,

Beware of false prophets, which come to you in sheep's clothing, but inwardly they are ravening wolves. Ye shall know them by their fruits. Do men gather grapes of thorns, or figs of thistles? Even so every good tree bringeth forth good fruit; but a corrupt tree bringeth forth evil fruit. A good tree cannot bring forth evil fruit, neither can a corrupt tree bring forth good fruit. Every tree that bringeth not forth good fruit is hewn down, and cast into the fire. Wherefore by their fruits ye shall know them.

These verses make it clear that the Knights Templar present a pseudo-Christianity that deludes many people.

[1]Nesta Webster, *Secret Societies*.

Four

Excerpts from the First Degree

❦

There are visible meanings given to a candidate or initiate in Masonry, and there are invisible or esoteric meanings behind the rituals. Each of the various steps in which an initiate must participate has given meanings, which are explained to the candidate. However, there is a reason as to why that particular step or mode was chosen in the first place. The invisible meanings are never revealed, and the only way to know them is to study what Masonic authorities have written about them.

First of all, there is the preparation of the candidate for initiation into the first degree of Freemasonry. The preparation takes place in a small room in the back of the main lodge room, where ministers, elders, and various other church leaders are among those preparing to become Masons.

The candidate is first deprived of all offensive and defensive weapons, divested of all clothing, and dressed in an old pair of trousers, blue in color, and a blue top with a "cable tow" around his neck. He is also blind-folded, or "hoodwinked," as Freemasonry terms it.

The only thing the candidate knows about the cable tow is what is told him in his obligations and lectures. It is a length of six feet used to measure the distance from shore his body will be buried after being mutilated should he betray the secrets of Masonry. It is part of his garment, and yet the meaning given the initiate is very simple.

The hidden meaning as to why the cable tow is used in the first place is found in the book entitled *Traditions of Freemasonry*, written by the well-known Masonic author Pierson, and which reads,

> In the mysteries of India, that is, in the secret worship of the pagan gods of India, the aspirant or candidate was invested with a consecrated sash or girdle which he was directed to wear next to his skin. It was manufactured with many myste-rious ceremonies, and said to possess the power of preserving the wearer from personal danger. It consisted of a cord composed of three times three threads twisted together and fastened at the end with a knot and was called a Zennar.

Hence comes the cable tow. On the high Masonic authority of Pierson, the Zennar of the Hindu initiation and the cable tow used in Freemasonry are one and the same, with coinciding features distinctly marked.

When the candidate stands at the anteroom door, he knocks three times. On the other side, the junior deacon also knocks three times and opens the door. He then says, "Who goes there?" The answer given by his conductor (the senior steward) is, "A poor blind candidate, who desires to be brought from darkness to light and receive a part of the rights and benefits of this right worshipful lodge, erected to God and dedicated to the Holy Saints John" (John the Baptist and John the evangelist).

Albert Mackey held the highest positions Masonry has to offer. He was a thirty-third degree Mason and Secretary General of the Supreme Council of the thirty-third degree Scottish Rite, a position he held for a great many years. In his *Manual of the Lodge,* he wrote,

> There he stands without our portals, on the threshold of his new Masonic life, in darkness, helplessness, and ignorance. Having been wandering amid the errors and covered over with the pollutions of the outer and profane world, he comes inquiringly to our door, seeking the new birth, and asking a withdrawal of the veil which conceals divine truth from his uninitiated sight.

In contrast, the Bible says in John 8:12 and John 9:5 that Jesus Christ is *"the light of the world"* and *"the light of life"* of men, keeping them from spiritual darkness. (See also Ephesians 5:14.)

As the candidate enters the lodge room, he is met by the senior deacon, who is holding a sharply pointed instrument to his breast, just short of piercing his skin. The deacon says to the candidate,

> Mr. ——, you are received into Masonry upon the point of a sharp instrument, piercing your naked (left) breast which is to teach you that as this is an instrument of torture to your flesh, so should the recollection thereof be to your conscience should you ever reveal any of the secrets of Freemasonry unlawfully.

In his manual, Albert Mackey also wrote of the ancient initiation, a secret worship of the pagan gods, in which the candidate was never permitted to enter on the threshold of the temple or sacred cavern in which ceremonies were conducted until, by the most solemn warnings, he had been impressed with the necessity of caution, secrecy, and fortitude.

The candidate is not told this hidden meaning. If he wants to know the meaning behind his movements and the reasons why they are employed, he must study the books written by eminent Masons who have researched the subject. Any Masonic library will carry the necessary books quoted herein. Certainly many Christians would leave Freemasonry if they understood the pagan nature of the rituals they practice and support.

Next, a prayer is given by the Worshipful Master with his hand upon the candidate's head as he kneels, while the lodge members stand:

> Vouchsafe Thine aid, almighty Father of the Universe, to this our present convention, and grant that this candidate for Masonry may dedicate and devote his life to Thy service, and become a true

and faithful brother among us. Endue him with a competency of Thy divine wisdom, that by the secrets of our art, he may be better enabled to display the beauties of holiness to the honor of Thy holy name. Amen.

With this prayer, they are asking God to bless a pagan ritual and to give the candidate the wisdom to use the satanic doctrines of Freemasonry to display the holiness of God.

The candidate then is conducted around the room, one circuit for each degree, in "search" of spiritual light. This journey around the room is called the *rite of circumambulation.*

This rite should alert the Christian candidate that he does not need this pseudo-spiritual light when he has Christ, who is the only true Light of men.

On page twenty-four of *Manual of the Lodge,* Albert Mackey wrote about the hidden meaning behind what is being done in this rite. He said, "The circumambulation among the pagan nations referred to the great doctrines of Sabaism, or sun worship." Freemasonry alone has preserved the primitive meaning, which was a symbolic allusion to the sun as the source of physical light and most wonderful work of the "Grand Architect of the Universe." The lodge represents the world. The three principal officers represent the sun in her three principal positions—at rising, at meridian, and at setting. The circumambulation alludes to the apparent course of the solar orbit through these points around the world.

Freemasonry

The candidate is then led to the base of the altar where a Holy Bible, square, and compass rest. The Worshipful Master instructs the candidate that he is about to take an oath or obligation and is assured it will not interfere with any duty he owes to God, his country, or himself.

When the candidate agrees to this, he is prepared and made to kneel at the altar, hand on the Bible, square, and compass, and he recites, as given, the oath of secrecy:

> I, ———, of my own free will and accord in presence of Almighty God and this right worshipful Lodge erected to Him and dedicated to the Holy Saints John, do hereby and hereon, do solemnly and sincerely promise and swear I will always hail, forever conceal, and never reveal any of the secret arts, parts, or points of the mysteries of Freemasonry which have been, may now, or shall hereafter be communicated to me in Charge as such, to any person in the world, except it be to a true and lawful brother free Mason, or in a legally constituted lodge of ancient free and accepted Masons, and not unto him nor them therein until after due trial, strict examination, or lawful information, I shall have found them legally entitled to receive the same. I, furthermore, promise and swear that I will not write, indite, print, paint, stamp, stain, cut, carve, mark, or engrave the same upon anything moveable or immovable under the canopy of heaven, whereby the least word, syllable, letter, or character thereof may become legible to myself or intelligible

to others, and the secrets of Freemasonry be unlawfully obtained, and that through my unworthiness. To all of which I solemnly and sincerely promise and swear to keep and perform the same, without any equivocation, mental reservation, or secret evasion of mind in me whatever, binding myself under no less a penalty than that of having my throat cut from ear to ear, my tongue torn out by its roots, and with my body buried in the rough sands of the sea, a cable's length from shore, where the tide ebbs and flows twice in twenty-four hours, should I ever knowingly or willingly violate this, my most solemn obligation as an entered apprentice, so help me God and keep me steadfast in the due performance of the same.

After promising this, he is asked to kiss the Bible one time as a seal and commitment to this oath. For each degree he will kiss the Bible in order to seal his commitment.

He must then ask the Worshipful Master for light (spiritually speaking) into the secrets of Freemasonry before he is allowed to see what is going on or receive any of the teachings, rights, or privileges. This is the first degree obligation of a Freemason, and the rest of his oaths, which could number from twelve or more, are much more binding with the death penalty.

Second Corinthians 6:14–16 states,

> Be ye not unequally yoked together with unbelievers: for what fellowship hath righteousness with unrighteousness? and what communion hath light with darkness?

and what concord hath Christ with Belial? or what part hath he that believeth with an infidel? and what agreement hath the temple of God with idols? for ye are the temple of the living God.

No one is required to take oaths to be found worthy to receive spiritual truths. All of the truth is in God's Word. Philippians 2:5 says, *"Let this mind be in you, which was also in Christ Jesus."* Also, 1 Corinthians 6:19-20 says,

What? know ye not that your body is the temple of the Holy Ghost which is in you, which ye have of God, and ye are not your own? For ye are bought with a price: therefore, glorify God in your body, and in your spirit, which are God's.

The Bible says in 2 Corinthians 11:14-15 that satan and his ministers appear as angels of light. This means that what they say sounds good, because they use biblical terminology. The Christian should be aware that the lodge teaches no truth from God's Word. Instead, it teaches a perverted gospel sprinkled with pseudo-religious ritual and biblical terminology.

Finally, brethren, whatsoever things are true, whatsoever things are honest, whatsoever things are just, whatsoever things are pure, whatsoever things are lovely, whatsoever things are of good report; if there be any virtue, and if there be any praise, think on these things. Those things, which ye have both learned, and received, and heard, and seen in me, do: and the God of peace shall be with you. (Philippians 4:8-9)

But I say unto you, Swear not at all; neither by heaven, for it is God's throne: nor by the earth; for it

is his footstool: neither by Jerusalem; for it is the city of the great King. Neither shalt thou swear by thy head, because thou canst not make one hair white or black. But let your communication be, Yea, yea; Nay, nay: for whatsoever is more than these cometh of evil.

(Matthew 5:34–37)

In order to pass from one degree to another in the first three degrees of Freemasonry, the initiate must memorize and recite by "word of mouth" what he went through and stand for examination in open lodge, where he is rejected or elected.

Here is a quote from a tract put out by the Grand Lodge of Maryland, received in 1976:

> Freemasonry is a kindness in the home, honesty in business, courtesy in society, fairness in work, pity and concern for the unfortunate, resistance toward evil, help for the weak, forgiveness for the penitent, love for one another, and above all, Freemasonry is a way of life.

Jesus is the example for Christians, but Freemasonry's way of life can, in no way, be compared to Christ's teachings. Freemasonry is in word opposed to evil; yet by its ritual, it is evil. The obligations, teachings, and penalties involved never include love and forgiveness as Jesus taught, nor do they reverence God. Instead, these rituals and doctrines mock God and disgrace the person and finished work of Christ. Dwight L. Moody once said that if a creed (or oath) does not lead a man to Christ, it is no creed at all.

First Degree Charge

The candidate stands at the altar, facing the Worshipful Master in the East, with the members and officers present. The senior deacon then delivers this charge to the candidate who has just received his first degree in Freemasonry and is now considered an Entered Apprentice Mason. This is the charge given:

Brother ———, as you are now introduced into the first principles of Masonry, we congratulate you on being accepted into the ancient and honorable Fraternity; ancient as having existed from time immemorial; and honoring as tending in every particular so to render all men who will be conformable to its precepts. No institution was ever raised on a better principle or more solid foundation, nor were ever more excellent rules and useful maxims laid down, than are inculcated in the several Masonic lectures. The greatest and best of men in all ages have been encouragers and promoters of the art, and they have never deemed it derogatory to their dignity to level themselves with the fraternity, extend their privileges and patronize their assemblies. There are three great duties, which as a Mason you are charged to inculcate: to God, to your neighbor and to yourself.

To God in never mentioning His name, but with that reverential awe which is due from a creature to his Creator, to implore His aid in all your laudable undertakings, and to esteem Him as the chief good; to your neighbor in acting upon the square, and doing unto him as you wish he should do unto you; and to yourself, in avoiding all irregularity and intemperance which may impair your faculties or debase the dignity of your profession. A zealous attachment to these duties will ensure public and private esteem. In the State you are to be a quiet and peaceful subject, true to your government, and just to your country. You are not to countenance disloyalty or rebellion, but patiently submit to legal authority and conform with cheerfulness to the government of the country in which you live. In your outward demeanor, be particularly careful to avoid censure and reproach. Although your frequent appearance at our regular meetings is earnestly solicited, yet it is not meant that Masonry should interfere with your necessary vocation, for these are on no account to be neglected, neither are you to suffer your zeal for the institution to lead you into argument with those who through ignorance may ridicule it. At your leisure hours, that you may improve in Masonic knowledge, you are to converse with well-informed brethren, who will be always as ready to give as you will be to receive instruction. Finally, keep sacred and inviolable the mysteries of the Fraternity, as these are to distinguish you from the rest of the community and mark your consequences among Masons. If, in the circle of your acquaintances, you find a person desirous of being initiated into Masonry, be particularly attentive not to recommend him unless you are convinced he will conform to our rules, that the honor, glory, and reputation of the institution may be firmly established, and the world at large convinced of its good effects.

The first part of this charge is the phrase, "No institution was ever raised on a better principle or more solid foundation, nor were ever more excellent rules and useful maxims laid down, than are inculcated in the several Masonic lectures."

First Corinthians 3:11 says, "*For other foundation can no man lay than that which is laid, which is Jesus Christ.*" Ask any Grand Lodge member in the world if the foundation of all Masonry's doctrines and beliefs is laid upon the Chief Cornerstone, Jesus Christ. There is no Masonic author who does not make a point in disassociating Freemasonry from Christianity. Masonry doctrine claims that the most excellent rules for conduct are found in the several Masonic lectures.

Mention is made that the candidate may, in his leisure hours, improve in Masonic knowledge; he is to converse with well-informed brethren who always will be as ready to give instruction as they are to receive it. God's Word says in Romans 12:1-2,

> I beseech you therefore, brethren, by the mercies of God, that ye present your bodies a living sacrifice, holy, acceptable unto God, which is your reasonable service. And be not conformed to this world: but be ye transformed, by the renewing of your mind, that ye may prove what is that good, and acceptable, and perfect, will of God.

Second Peter 3:18 reads, "*But grow in grace, and in the knowledge of our Lord and Saviour, Jesus Christ.*"

The Bible teaches that the improvement of knowledge should be in Christ Jesus, which results in the transformation of our minds and wills. Freemasonry seeks to assure that the candidate converses only with Masonic brethren when seeking truths. After a period of time and much repetitive teaching, satan has masterminded a seared conscience, harder than brass and unable to discern a truth from a lie.

There is another point to discuss in this charge. It says, "If, in the circle of your acquaintances, you find a person desirous of being initiated into Masonry, be particularly attentive not to recommend him unless you are convinced he will conform to our rules, that the honor, glory, and reputation of the institution may be firmly established, and the world at large, convinced of its good effects." It is impossible to be convinced the person you recommend for Masonry will be conformed to rules and regulations he cannot know until he has been obligated by oath. Once saturated with Masonic doctrine, one's soul and spirit become numb to truth, until he has renounced his error before God.

A large portion of the Congress and Senate, judges, governors, mayors, and legislature belongs to Masonry. The effects of secular humanism are rather horrifying. In 2 Timothy 3, the effect such teachings have on men in high places is exposed and can be seen operating in these last days prior to the rapture of the church. Some people question the opposition to Freemasonry over and above other cults such as Jehovah's Witnesses, Mormonism, and Christian Science. It is the only cult on this earth that has penetrated the pulpit and spiritual sessions of our churches.

Freemasonry's doctrinal beliefs and practices will be one of satan's major tools in forming the one-world apostate church during the Great Tribulation.

Random Excerpts from the First Degree Lecture

The following are descriptions of the furniture in King Solomon's temple, as given to the Mason. They are excerpted from the *Maryland Masonic Manual*:

Covering (Referring to the lodge room)

> Its covering is no less than the clouded canopy or starry-decked Heaven, where all good Masons hope, at last, to arrive by aid of the theological ladder which Jacob in his vision saw extending from earth to Heaven. The three principal rounds of this ladder are denominated Faith, Hope, and Charity, which admonishes us to have Faith in God, Hope in immortality, and Charity to all mankind. The greatest of these is Charity; for Faith may be lost in sight, Hope ends in fruition, but Charity extends beyond the grave through the boundless realms of Eternity.

Furniture

> The furniture of a lodge is the Holy Bible, the Square, and the Compasses. The Holy Bible is dedicated to God, because it is the inestimable gift of God to man and on it a Mason is obligated; the Square to the Master, because it is the proper

Masonic emblem of his office; and the Compasses to the Craft, because, by due attention to their use, Masons are taught to circumscribe their desires and keep their passions within due bounds.

Ornaments

The ornaments of a lodge are the Mosaic Pavement, the Indented Tessel, and the Blazing Star. The Mosaic Pavement is a representation of the ground floor of King Solomon's temple. It is also emblematic of human life, checkered with good and evil. The Indented Tessel, that beautiful tessellated border, or skirting which surrounds it, is emblematic of those manifold blessings and comforts which surround the Masons, and which they hope to enjoy by faithful reliance on Divine Providence, which is hieroglyphically represented by the Blazing Star in the center.

Dedication

Lodges are dedicated to King Solomon, who was the first Most Excellent Grand Master; yet Masons professing Christianity dedicate theirs to St. John the Baptist and St. John the Evangelist, who were two eminent Christian Patrons of Masonry: and since their time is represented in every regular and well-governed Lodge, a certain point within a circle, bordered by two perpendicular parallel lines representing St. John the Baptist and St. John the Evangelist: and upon the top rests the Holy Scriptures. The point represents an individual brother; the circle, that boundary line beyond which he should never suffer his prejudices or passions to betray him. In going around this circle we necessarily touch upon these two parallel lines as well as the Holy Scriptures; and while a Mason keeps himself circumscribed within Masonic precepts, it is impossible that he should materially err.

Tenets of Profession

The Tenets of our profession are Brotherly Love, Relief, and Truth.

Brotherly Love

By the exercise of Brotherly Love, we are taught to regard the whole human species as one family; the high and low, the rich and poor, who, as created by one Almighty Parent, and inhabitants of the same planet, are to aid, support, and protect each other. On this principle Masonry unites men of every country, sect, and opinion, and conciliates true friendship among those who might otherwise have remained at a perpetual distance.

Fortitude

Fortitude is that noble and steady purpose of mind whereby we are enabled to undergo any pain, peril, or danger, when prudentially deemed expedient. This virtue is equally distant from rashness and cowardice, and, like the former, should be deeply impressed upon your mind as a safeguard or security against any illegal attack that may be made by force, or otherwise, to extort from you any of those valuable secrets with which you have been so solemnly entrusted, and which were emblematically represented upon your first admission into the Lodge.

Justice

Justice is that standard or boundary of right which enables us to render to every man his just due without distinction. This virtue is not only consistent with Divine and human laws, but is the very cement and support of civil society. And as justice in a great measure constitutes the real good man, so should it be your invariable practice, never to deviate from the minutest principles thereof.

The meanings given the Mason to each of the excerpts of the first degree lecture are not for the Christian. They use biblical terminology but never proper biblical interpretation. All their explanations mention God in abstract, never as God of the Bible. They use character building, not faith in the living Christ, to guide and govern their lives. Second Peter 2:1–3 says,

> But there were false prophets also among the people, even as there shall be false teachers among you, who secretly shall bring in damnable heresies, even denying the Lord that bought them, and bring upon themselves swift destruction. And many shall follow their pernicious ways, by reason of whom the way of truth shall be evil spoken of. And through covetousness shall they with feigned words make merchandise of you: whose judgment now of a long time lingereth not, and their damnation slumbereth not.

Ephesians 3:16-19 says,

> That he would grant you, according to the riches of
> his glory, to be strengthened with might by his Spirit in
> the inner man; that Christ may dwell in your hearts by
> faith; that ye, being rooted and grounded in love, may be
> able to comprehend with all saints what is the breadth,
> and length, and depth, and height; and to know the love
> of Christ, which passeth knowledge, that ye might be
> filled with all the fulness of God.

***

The following section will examine the Immovable
Jewels of Freemasonry as defined in the *Maryland
Masonic Manual*.

Immovable Jewels

The immovable jewels are the Rough Ashlar,
the Perfect Ashlar, and the Trestle Board. The
Rough Ashlar is a stone as taken from the quarry
in its rude and natural state. The Perfect Ashlar is a
stone made ready by the hands of the workmen, to
be adjusted by the working tools of the Fellowcraft.
The Trestle Board is for the master workmen to use
to draw his designs. By the Rough Ashlar we are
reminded of our rude and imperfect state by nature.
By the Perfect Ashlar, we are reminded of that state
of perfection at which we hope to arrive, by a virtuous education, our own endeavors, and the blessing
of God. By the Trestle Board, we are also reminded
that, as the operative workman erects his temporal
building agreeably to the rules and designs laid

down by the master on his Trestle Board, so should we endeavor to erect our spiritual building agreeably to the rules and designs laid down by the Supreme Architect of the Universe in the great books of nature and revelation. This is our spiritual, moral, and Masonic Trestle Board.

There are two things to always remember about Masonic teaching that are extremely important and absolutely necessary to the understanding of the mind of this cult.

The most important fact is that Masonry never reveals the root cause of the reason man is imperfect. Man is imperfect because of the fall of man; our sinful nature is inherited from Adam. The word *sin* is impossible to find in Masonry, except in the Knights Templar lodge, and there it is used in an unscriptural manner.

The second fact not communicated is the biblical solution to the problem of man's imperfect state.

A close examination will reveal Masonry's falling short of God's standard. Masonic doctrine says, "By the Perfect Ashlar we are reminded of the state of perfection at which we hope to arrive by...." The word *by* is the key in this statement. It indicates that Masonry is going to explain how to arrive at the state of perfection, that is, how to correct what is rude and imperfect by nature.

The statement continues, "At which we hope to arrive by a virtuous education, our own endeavors, and the blessing of God." Masonry teaches that a virtuous education partially corrects the sinful nature. And what is this virtuous education? It is study in the arts and sciences of the world. This is not God's way of eradicating the sinful nature.

The second method Freemasonry employs to change this imperfect state to a perfect one is by personal endeavors. God's Word never promotes self-effort or good works to achieve salvation or perfection of character.

The third step in arriving at that state of perfection in Masonry is by the blessing of God. But God cannot give His blessing to a doctrinal system that promotes human perfection in place of the blood of Jesus Christ. God's blessing is contingent upon a proper relationship with His Son. He never blesses that which is contrary to His holy and perfect nature.

Masonic doctrine goes on to say one should, by the symbol of the Trestle Board, erect his spiritual building agreeably to the rules and designs laid down by the Supreme Architect of the Universe in the great books of nature and revelation.

The Lord Jesus Christ is the Chief Cornerstone and Foundation of the spiritual building, as declared in Ephesians 2:20–22 and 1 Peter 2:5, but Masonry ignores Him. Masonry replaces Christ with the symbol of a Trestle Board.

Masonry's definition of the great books of nature and revelation is any sacred book of most world religions as revealed to them in their pagan beliefs.

Albert Mackey stated in his book *Encyclopedia of Freemasonry*, under the heading of "Bible,"

The Bible is used among Masons as the symbol of the will of God, however it may be expressed, and therefore, whatever to any people expresses that will may be used as a substitute for the Bible in a Masonic Lodge. Thus in a lodge consisting of Jews, the Old Testament alone may be used upon the altar, while Turkish Masons may use the Koran. Whether it be the Gospels to the Christians, the Pentateuch to the Israelites, the Vedas to the Brahman, it everywhere conveys the same idea, that of the symbolism of the Divine Will revealed to men.

Under the heading of "Scripture" in the same book we read,

Although in Christendom very few Masons deny the divine authority of the Scriptures of the Old and New Testaments, yet to require as a preliminary to initiation, the declaration of such a belief, is directly in opposition to the express regulation of the order, which demands a belief in God and, by implication, in the immortality of the soul as the only religious test.

We are told that the great books of nature and revelation are the Mason's spiritual, moral, and Masonic Trestle Board. The Christian's spiritual and moral Trestle Board is the person of Jesus Christ. The Christian is empowered by the Holy Spirit who is called, in John's gospel, *the Spirit of truth* (John 14:17). According to Masonry, as the Mason increases in knowledge and wisdom, and works hard at moral purity or perfection,

God will bless him with having arrived at a state of perfection! This is a satanically oriented plan of salvation, to say the least. Paul stated in 2 Corinthians 5:17, *"Therefore if any man be in Christ, he is a new creature: old things are passed away; behold, all things are become new."* Man's sinful, rude state is actually perfected in Christ Jesus by accepting Him as Savior and Lord. The Bible further states in 1 John 1:6–7,

> If we say that we have fellowship with him, and walk in darkness, we lie, and do not the truth: but if we walk in the light, as he is in the light, we have fellowship one with another, and the blood of Jesus Christ his Son cleanseth us from all sin.

Masonry declares that character determines man's destiny. But God declares that His grace and man's faith determine man's destiny.

Truth

According to the *Maryland Masonic Manual*, truth is a "divine attribute" and "the foundation of every virtue." It further says,

> To be good and true is the first lesson we are taught in Masonry. On this theme we contemplate, and by its dictates endeavor to regulate our conduct: hence, while influenced by this principle, hypocrisy and deceit are unknown among us, sincerity and plain dealing distinguish us, and the heart and tongue join in promoting each other's welfare, and in rejoicing in each other's prosperity.

Simply stated, the definition of the word *virtue* is moral excellence, purity of life, or perfection of character. Masonry says that truth is behind every virtue. Jesus said in John 14:6 that He is *"the way, the truth, and the life."* Jesus is truth, the foundation of all virtue and moral purity in a person. In Romans 3:10–13, God describes the total depravity of the whole human race:

> As it is written, There is none righteous, no, not one: there is none that understandeth, there is none that seeketh after God....There is none that doeth good, no, not one. Their throat is an open sepulchre; with their tongues they have used deceit; the poison of asps is under their lips.

Further on in that chapter, the answer to removing this curse upon all mankind is found:

> Even the righteousness of God which is by faith of Jesus Christ unto all and upon all them that believe: for there is no difference: for all have sinned, and come short of the glory of God; being justified freely by his grace through the redemption that is in Christ Jesus.
>
> (Romans 3:22–24)

Also note Romans 5:1, which states, *"Therefore, being justified by faith, we have peace with God through our Lord Jesus Christ."* Romans 8:29 tells us to be conformed as Christians to the image of Christ. Jesus said a man cannot serve two masters (Matthew 6:24). First Corinthians 15:33 says, *"Do not be deceived: 'Evil company corrupts good habits'"* (NKJV). Masonry has taken truth, combined it with false doctrine, and held it as absolute truth. An old axiom says, "A half of a truth told as a whole truth is a whole lie."

Masonry is a collection of the pagan rites, initiations, and religions of Egypt, and the worship of the sun god, sprinkled with enough biblical terminology to deceive the unsuspecting. Its definition of truth originated with satan in the Garden of Eden. The entire account in Genesis shows how satan deliberately deceived Eve and perpetuated a lie to her, but made it appear to be the truth. The Christian Mason should test the spirits as John commanded in 1 John 5. He should read the lodge manual, listen carefully to all of the rituals and meanings, and then ask for the reasons and interpretations of why candidates move the way they do in the lodge room and how the various forms of rituals came about. When he has done this, he should compare everything with the Word of God.

Temperance

The following definition is from the *Maryland Masonic Manual*.

> Temperance is that due restraint upon our affections and passions which renders the body tame and governable, and frees the mind from the allurements of vice. This virtue should be your constant practice, as you are thereby taught to avoid excess, or contracting any licentious or vicious habit, the indulgence of which might lead you to disclose some of those valuable secrets which you have promised to conceal and never reveal, and which would

consequently subject you to the contempt and detestation of all good Masons.

In connection with the idea of temperance, allow me to present some of the penalties given at the end of the oaths of various degrees in Masonry. They are the first and third degree penalties, the penalties of the Knights of Malta, Scottish Rite in the tenth degree, and the Shrine. The oaths that precede these penalties are not given because of their length. The penalties will reveal just how Masonry practices temperance.

No. 1—First Degree Penalty

Under no less a penalty than that of having my throat cut from ear to ear, my tongue torn out by its roots, and with my body buried in the rough sands of the sea, a cable length from shore, where the tide ebbs and flows twice in twenty-four hours, should I ever knowingly or willingly violate this, my solemn obligation as an Entered Apprentice, so help me God, and keep me steadfast in the due performance of the same.

No. 2—Third Degree Penalty

Under no less a penalty than that of having my body severed in twain, my bowel taken thence, and with my body burned to ashes, and those ashes scattered to the four winds of heaven, so that there might remain name, trace, nor remembrance of so vile a wretch as I would be, should I ever knowingly or willingly violate this, my most solemn obligation, as a Master Mason, so help me God, and keep me steadfast in the due performance of the same.

No. 3—Knights of Malta

After taking the upper part of a human skull in the hand, the following penalty is repeated after the Grand Commander.

This pure wine I now take in testimony of my belief in the mortality of the body and the immortality of the soul, and may this libation appear as a witness against me both here and hereafter. And as the sins of the world were laid upon the head of the Savior, so may all the sins committed by the person whose skull this was be heaped upon my head, in addition to my own, should I ever knowingly or willingly violate or transgress any obligation that I have heretofore taken, take at this time, or shall at any future period take in relation to any degree of Masonry or order of Knighthood. So help me God.

No. 4—Tenth Degree—Scottish Rite

And in failure of this my obligation, I consent to have my body opened perpendicularly, and to be exposed for eight hours in the open air, that the venomous flies may eat of my entrails, my head to be cut off and put on the highest pinnacle of the world, and I will always be ready to inflict the same punishment on those who shall disclose this degree and break this obligation. So help me God and maintain me, Amen.

No. 5—Shrine A.A.O.N.M.S.

In willful violation whereof I may incur the fearful penalty of having my eyeballs pierced to the center with a three-edged blade, my feet flayed, and I be forced to walk the hot sands upon the sterile shores of the Red Sea, until the flaming sun shall strike me with livid plague, and my Allah the God of Arab Muslim and Mohammedan, the God of our fathers support me to the entire fulfillment of the same. Amen, Amen, Amen.

These penalties are secret rituals and are given via word of mouth only.

Masonry states in the first sentence of the definition of temperance that it is a "due restraint upon affections and passions, which render the body tame and governable and frees the mind from the allurements of vice." On one hand, Masonry encourages one to exercise temperance, and then on the other insists not only one's body be mutilated upon exposure of rituals and purposes, but that he take part in doing the same to others.

This virtue of temperance should be one's constant practice, as one is thereby taught to avoid excess or contracting any licentious or vicious habit. What could be more vicious than the penalties, rituals, and teachings of Freemasonry? Freemasonry also gives the reason why one is not to contract any vicious habit. It is not because of concern about an individual's well-being, or that of his family. Rather, it is because the indulgence of such might lead him to disclose some of those valuable secrets he has promised to conceal. Of course, Masonry does not want the world, especially the Christian community, to behold or have the opportunity to discern the actual rituals of Masonry.

The teachings of Freemasonry condition the mind in areas that should have already been occupied by the person of Jesus Christ. Its teachings not only condition, but also blind, the minds of men to the real truth in every area of life.

Such revelation of the secrets of Masonry due to lack of restraint on the part of any member would consequently subject him to the contempt and detestation of all good Masons. A good Mason is supposed to show detestation to those who have renounced the order. If a man does not show detestation, he is a poor Mason. What is the meaning, in simple terms, of these words *contempt* and *detestation?*

Contempt means to scorn (something the Pharisees did to Jesus at His trial). Detestation means extreme dislike, to abhor or loathe. But God's Word says in Romans 8:1, *"There is therefore now no condemnation to them which are in Christ Jesus, who walk not after the flesh, but after the Spirit."*

Prudence

This is Masonry's definition of prudence, according to the *Maryland Masonic Manual:*

Prudence teaches us to regulate our lives and actions agreeably to the dictates of reason, and is that habit by which we wisely judge, and prudentially determine on all things relative to our present as well as to our future happiness. This virtue should be your peculiar characteristic, not only for the government of your conduct while in the Lodge, but also when abroad in the world. It should be particularly attended to in all strange and mixed companies, never to let fall the least sign, token, or word whereby the secrets of Freemasonry might be unlawfully obtained.

Again, the Mason is reminded, at the end of these explanations of the consequences, of the oath he took if he should ever betray his trust.

Prudence teaches a Mason how to regulate his life "agreeably to the dictates of reason." Quoted is a part of the definition of *reasoning* from Webster's dictionary: "Reason is that mental faculty in man, which enables him to deduce inferences from fact, and to distinguish right from wrong; right judgment, right thinking." The dictionary also says, "Human reasoning based on human input, exercising according to human ability." Never is a Mason told in the explanation that his reasoning is to be controlled by God. Never is he told that an ability to think or judge rightly must come from a proper relationship with Jesus Christ.

Man cannot judge right from wrong or reason without pollution, apart from divine guidance. Man judges according to instincts, rules, and laws. Romans 3 reveals the total depravity of mankind, including his inability to reason or to be prudent. Since the Garden of Eden, man is not prudent unless he is controlled by a higher and holier power than himself. This power is Jehovah God, the great "I Am," and has, in these last days, been manifested and revealed to mankind through the person of Jesus Christ.

Masonry goes on to say that prudence is that habit by which we wisely judge and determine all things relative to our present, as well as our future, happiness. A Christian's present has been settled at Calvary, and his happiness in the present is declared in God's Word as his new life in Christ Jesus. His future happiness is, according to God's Word, so wonderful that it is beyond the thoughts, heart, and mind of man. God gives us glimpses of future happiness in His Word, especially in the book of Revelation. God's Word alone determines the rule for judgment in all things.

If everything in Christianity were leveled to the comprehension of reason, there would be no room for faith. It is better to believe humbly than to reason presumptuously. Those reasonings may be called presumptuous because they lead to the denial of the immutability of divine counsel. Denying the freedom of the human will and making man a machine also makes God the author of sin. Christians live by faith, not by corrupted reasoning.

Masonry continues in telling us that this virtue should be the peculiar characteristic of men, not only in the lodge, but in the world. Why are Masons told to be prudent in the world? It is so that they will (according to their definition of prudence) never reveal the least sign, token, or word whereby the secrets of Freemasonry might be unlawfully obtained.

Truth, such as God presents it through His Son Jesus Christ, is open for all to behold and evaluate. Satan is the prince of darkness, so he manifests himself in anything that can be hidden from true biblical discernment. Jesus said in John 18:20, *"I spoke openly to the world; I ever taught in the synagogue, and in the temple, whither the Jews always resort; and in secret have I said nothing."* Freemasonry cannot make the same claim.

Humanism is works and self-deification, as is Freemasonry. Christianity is faith.

Five

Excerpts from the
Second Degree

The obligation or oath of a second degree Mason (Fellowcraft) is as follows:

I, ———, of my own free will and accord, in presence of Almighty God, and this right worship-ful Lodge erected to Him, and dedicated to the Holy Saints John, do hereby and hereon, solemnly and sincerely, promise and swear, I will always hail, for-ever conceal, and never reveal, any of the secret arts, parts, or points of the mysteries of the Fellowcraft degree, which have been, may now, or shall hereaf-ter be communicated to me, in charge as such, to any person in the world, except it be to a true and lawful brother Fellowcraft, and not unto him, nor them therein, until after due trial, strict examina-tion, or lawful information, I shall have found them legally entitled to receive the same. I further-more promise and swear, that I will stand to and abide by the rules and regulations of the Fellowcraft lodge, of which I may be a member. I furthermore

71

promise and swear that I will not wrong a brother Fellowcraft. To all of which, I solemnly and sincerely may be a member. I furthermore promise and swear to keep and perform the same, without any equivocation, mental reservation, or secret evasion of mind in me whatever, binding myself under no less a penalty than that of having my left breast torn open, my heart plucked out, and with my body left to the vultures of the air, should I ever knowingly or willingly violate this, my most solemn obligation, as a Fellowcraft, so help me, God, and keep me steadfast in the due performance of the same.

The brother is now made to kiss the Bible twice to seal his commitment to his oath.

The Scriptures used to refute taking first degree oaths apply here also.

Speculative Masonry

The *Maryland Masonic Manual* records the explanation of speculative Masonry as it is given to the candidate for the second degree:

It is so far interwoven with religion as to lay us under obligation to pay that rational homage to the Deity which at once constitutes our duty and our happiness. It leads the contemplative to view with reverence and admiration the glorious works of creation, and inspires him with the most exalted ideas of the perfection of his divine Creator.

Also according to the *Manual*, through speculative Masonry the initiate learns to "subdue the passions, act upon the square, keep a tongue of good report, maintain secrecy, and practice charity."

First, the Mason is to keep a tongue of good report and practice charity. In the third chapter of James, we read,

> And the tongue is a fire, a world of iniquity: so is the tongue among our members, that it defileth the whole body, and setteth on fire the course of nature; and it is set on fire of hell. (James 3:6)

The tongue of man should never utter God's name in such blasphemous rituals and repeat in catechisms such satanic doctrines as are employed in the various Masonic degrees.

In the first degree charge, the initiate is told that if he renounces Freemasonry, he will suffer the contempt and detestation of all good Masons. Try having contempt and hostility for someone without using your tongue! Masonry operates on the principle of situation ethics. In its teaching on charity, it is obvious from its rituals that charity extends primarily to other Masons or relatives. There is no doubt that Freemasonry strays from the true meaning of biblical love that is outlined in 1 Corinthians 13.

Next, the initiate is told to subdue the passions and act upon the square. Speculative Freemasonry, as practiced today, is supposed to accomplish this. As Christians, any effort we make to subdue passions or the sinful nature can only come about as they are put under the absolute control of the Holy Spirit. Romans 8:37 says, *"We are more than conquerors through him that loved us."* The *"him that loved us"* refers to Jesus Christ. It is through Him that we are conquerors in this world in all circumstances, even over our sinful natures. God through His Son calls people out of the world system, under the control of satan, into the kingdom of His Son Jesus Christ. In John 17:14, in His high priestly prayer, Christ stated, *"I have given them thy word; and the world hath hated them, because they are not of the world, even as I am not of the world."* He calls people out of the world system to serve the living God.

To try to subdue the passions with human effort and discipline, apart from the person and finished work of Christ, as Masonry does, is fruitless, and will always end in failure. Self-exaltation through self-effort is satanic, not biblical. Acting upon the square, according to Albert G. Mackey in his book *Encyclopedia of Freemasonry*, is summed up in one sentence: "The square is a symbol of morality, of truthfulness and honesty."

How can Masonry teach its adherents to be honest and truthful when everything it teaches is contrary to God's Word? A lie cannot be the truth. Masonry cannot admonish anyone to be honest and truthful in acting upon the square, when all it teaches and practices is completely isolated from the person and finished work of Jesus Christ.

Romans chapter three outlines the absolute depravity of all mankind. Thus, total depravity exists until the individual person has accepted Jesus Christ as Savior and Lord. Until then, any honesty and truthfulness is satanic and under satan's control, and the unbeliever is under the wrath of God.

When studying Masonic teaching, one must always look at those standards to which it is applying the principles it teaches. If it is not Christian in its entirety, and if it does not give glory to Jesus Christ exclusively, it can then only give glory to man or the devil or both. Remember, self-effort and self-discipline apart from Christ equals self-deification.

The Mason is admonished to maintain secrecy. Are the doctrines and mysteries of the Word of God to be kept secret from the world? In Matthew 28, Jesus commanded the disciples to go into all the world and preach the Gospel, the Good News. Freemasonry says that its mysteries are to be kept secret. The reason is that it does not want the world, especially the Christian community, to have a chance to evaluate the real and true character of this cult.

The next statement made is that speculative Masonry is so far interwoven with religion "as to lay us under obligation to pay the rational homage to the Deity which at once constitutes duty and happiness." But Freemasonry does not specify as to which religion speculative Masonry is so far "interwoven." It could be anything or everything or nothing by this definition.

The religion with which Freemasonry is so far interwoven is its own, the god of which is the god of naturalism.

Masonry's basic teaching is humanistic. If the religion of Freemasonry was deeply interwoven with Christianity, it would not be Freemasonry. If it was deeply interwoven with Islam, Judaism, Hinduism, or Mormonism, it would be one of those. But Freemasonry considers its religion universal.

Masonry also states that Masons should pay rational homage to the deity that constitutes duty and happiness. This Masonic deity is quite different from the biblical God, Jehovah.

John 4:23 says, *"But the hour cometh, and now is, when the true worshippers shall worship the Father in spirit and in truth: for the Father seeketh such to worship him."*

Moral Advantages of Geometry

An explanation of the letter G over the Master's chair in the East is given the brother of second degree:

> Geometry, the first and noblest of sciences, is the basis upon which the superstructure of Masonry is erected. By Geometry we may curiously trace nature through her various windings to her most concealed recesses. By it, we may discover the power, the wisdom, and the goodness of the Grand Artificer of the Universe, and view with delight the proportions which connect this vast machine. By it, we may discover how the planets move in their different orbits and demonstrate their various revolutions. By it, we account for the return of seasons and the variety of scenes which each season displays to the discerning eye. Numberless worlds are

around us, all framed by the same Divine Artist, which roll through the vast expanse, and are all conducted by the same unerring law of nature. A survey of nature and the observation of her beautiful proportions, first determined man to imitate the Divine plan, and study symmetry and order. This gave rise to society and birth to every useful art. The architect began to design, and the plans which he laid down, being improved by experience and time, have produced works which are the admiration of every age. The lapse of time, the ruthless hand of ignorance, and the devastations of war, have laid waste and destroyed many valuable monuments of antiquity on which the utmost exertions of human genius have been employed. Even the Temple of Solomon, so spacious and magnificent and constructed by so many celebrated artists, escaped not the unsparing ravages of barbarous force. Freemasonry, notwithstanding, has still survived. The attentive Ear receives the sound from the instructive Tongue, and the secrets of Freemasonry are safely lodged in the repository of the faithful Breast. Tools and instruments of architecture, and symbolic emblems most expressive, wise and expressive, are selected by the Fraternity to imprint on the mind serious truths; and thus, through a succession of ages, are transmitted unimpaired, the most excellent tenets of our Institution.

To impress this explanation on the minds of its members, initiates are told that the letter G (between the square and compass emblem worn by most Masons on rings and lapel pins) represents, first, the science of geometry, and, second, the sacred name of the deity. One is not told which of the many deities, worshipped by the hundreds of religions of the world, that G represents. That option is left to the individual. It just represents god in whatever way he happens to manifest himself to the individual.

The world has three evidences of the revelation of God: first, in nature; second, in the written Word; and, third, in God's Son, Jesus Christ. When God is noticed in nature, it is meant to point mankind to the truth of who God is and how He is revealed in and through the person of Jesus Christ and His Word. Freemasonry cannot do this, since Masonry accepts the deities of many religions.

Thereby, knowing that there is a person, Jesus Christ, who has been declared to the world to be the Savior, Masonry rejects Him and continues its own pagan representation of God, known as the Grand Architect of the Universe.

Masonry's god is a force in nature, not a personal "Supreme Being." If he were a personal god, then he would be named or identified in one of the world's religions, but he is not. This is a master deception to all who join and yoke up with this satanic deity of Masonry.

Ye are my witnesses, saith the LORD, and my servant whom I have chosen: that ye may know and believe me, and understand that I am he: before me there was no God formed, neither shall there be after me. I, even I,

am the LORD; and beside me there is no saviour. I have declared, and have saved, and I have showed, when there was no strange god among you: therefore ye are my witnesses, saith the LORD, that I am God. Yea, before the day was I am he; and there is none that can deliver out of my hand: I will work, and who shall let it?
(Isaiah 43:10–13)

And she shall bring forth a son, and thou shalt call his name JESUS: for he shall save his people from their sins. Now all this was done, that it might be fulfilled which was spoken of the Lord by the prophet, saying, Behold, a virgin shall be with child, and shall bring forth a son, and they shall call his name Emmanuel, which being interpreted is God with us. (Matthew 1:21–23)

But unto the Son he saith, Thy throne, O God, is for ever and ever: a sceptre of righteousness is the sceptre of thy kingdom. (Hebrews 1:8)

I am Alpha and Omega, the beginning and the ending, saith the Lord, which is, and which was, and which is to come, the Almighty. (Revelation 1:8)

Then Paul stood in the midst of Mars' hill, and said, Ye men of Athens, I perceive that in all things ye are too superstitious. For as I passed by, and beheld your devotions, I found an altar with this inscription, TO THE UNKNOWN GOD. Whom therefore ye ignorantly worship, him declare I unto you. (Acts 17:22–23)

All things were made by him; and without him was not any thing made that was made. (John 1:3)

*But to us there is but one God, the Father, of whom are
all things, and we in him; and one Lord Jesus Christ,
by whom are all things, and we by him.*

(1 Corinthians 8:6)

*For by him were all things created, that are in heaven,
and that are in earth, visible and invisible, whether they
be thrones, or dominions, or principalities, or powers: all
things were created by him, and for him.*

(Colossians 1:16)

*God, who at sundry times and in divers manners spake
in time past unto the fathers by the prophets, hath in
these last days spoken unto us by his Son, whom he
hath appointed heir of all things, by whom also he made
the worlds.*　　　　　　　　(Hebrews 1:1-2)

Masonry does not point to Jesus Christ as the Grand
Artificer of the Universe (G.A.O.T.U.) mentioned in
their lecture.

Second Half of Second Degree Charge

Here is a direct quote of part of the second degree
charge, taken from the *Manual*:

The study of the liberal arts, that valuable
branch of education which tends so effectually to
polish and adorn the mind, is earnestly recommended to your consideration, especially the science of geometry, which is established as the basis
of our art. Geometry, or Masonry, originally synon-
ymous terms, being of a divine and moral nature,
is enriched with the most useful knowledge. While

it proves the wonderful properties of nature, it demonstrates the more important truths of morality. Your past behavior and regular deportment have merited the honor which we have now conferred; and in your new character, it is expected that you will conform to the principles of the Fraternity by steadily persevering in the practice of every commendable virtue. Such is the nature of your engagement as a Fellowcraft, and to these duties you are bound by the most sacred ties.

The study of the liberal arts, especially the science of geometry, is earnestly recommended because "it polishes the mind." Should believers concentrate on liberal arts and the science of geometry? In this charge, geometry, or Masonry, is "enriched with the most useful knowledge." Masonry is not interested in the commands set forth in God's Word for Christians to grow in the knowledge of our Lord and Savior Jesus Christ. Masonry wants the initiate to spend his time on the effects of creation and nature, and from these draw deep moral fibers, while making sure he does not see the cause behind the effects.

The real cause of all things is Jesus Christ, not a god of the numerous religions of the world. There is only one true and living God of all the universe, and He has been revealed to the people of the earth in the person of Jesus Christ, true God and true man. He is not some abstract idea or principle out in space.

John 17:3 states, *"And this is life eternal, that they might know thee the only true God, and Jesus Christ, whom thou hast sent."* This teaching is not vague. When God speaks, His voice is clear and concise. When satan speaks, his mouth is full of lies and deceits. Jesus said so in John 8:44.

Continuing in this charge, the initiate is told that while Masonry proves the wonderful properties of nature, it demonstrates the more important truth of morality. It is referring to the science of geometry. However, all the important truths of morality for mankind are given in the Word of God as contained in both the Old and New Testaments, not in the science of geometry or nature or the Masonic code of ethics, symbolized here by geometry.

Regardless of how hidden the meanings behind these statements are, or how the Mason takes them, they result in a code of ethics completely contrary to God's Word.

The initiate is told that in his new character he is expected to conform to the principles of Freemasonry by steadily persevering in the practice of every commendable virtue. That expression, *new character*, has profound meaning in Freemasonry. As a Mason, he is expected to represent this cult in all of its beliefs and doctrines. He is held by his oath, committed by a most sacred vow to give complete loyalty to Freemasonry and all for which it stands.

> *This I say then, Walk in the Spirit, and ye shall not fulfil the lust of the flesh. For the flesh lusteth against the Spirit, and the Spirit against the flesh: and these are contrary the one to the other: so that ye cannot do the*

*things that ye would. But if ye be led of the Spirit, ye are
not under the law.* (Galatians 5:16–18)

Two Pillars

When the two pillars are set up about five to six feet
apart, the senior deacon brings the new initiate into the
lodge room (via the anteroom door) and closes the door.
He puts the initiate in a straight line next to the anteroom door and says,

> Brethren, Masonry is here considered under
> two denominations, operative and speculative. By
> operative Masonry, we allude to a proper applica-
> tion of the useful rules of architecture, whence a
> structure will derive figure, strength, and beauty,
> and when will result a due proportion and a just
> correspondence in all its parts. It furnishes us with
> dwellings and convenient shelters from the vicissi-
> tudes and inclemencies of the seasons; and while
> it displays the effects of human wisdom, as well
> as the choice, as in the arrangement of the sundry
> materials of which an edifice is composed, it dem-
> onstrates that a fund of science and industry is
> implanted in man for the best, most salutory and
> beneficial purposes. By speculative Masonry, we
> learn to subdue the passions, act upon the square,
> keep a tongue of good report, maintain secrecy,
> and practice charity. It is so far interwoven with
> religion, as to lay us under obligation to pay that
> rational homage to the Deity which at once consti-
> tutes our duty and our happiness. It leads the con-
> templative to view with reverence and admiration

the glorious works of creation, and inspires him with the most exalted ideas of the perfection of his Divine Creator.

The senior deacon then takes the initiate's arm, assisted by the steward, and says, "Brethren we are now about to make our approach by an imaginary flight of winding stairs consisting of three, five, and seven steps, to a place representing the middle chamber of King Solomon's temple." He then says to the initiate he is conducting,

> The first objects that attract our attention upon our approach are these two pillars, set up in front of the porch of King Solomon's temple. The one on the right, the other on the left. The one on the left is called Boaz, and signifies strength; the one on the right, Jachin, and signifies to establish. In strength I shall establish my kingdom. These pillars were thirty and five cubits in height and were adorned with chapters of five cubits, making forty cubits. They were adorned with lily work, net work, and pomegranates, denoting peace, unity, and plenty. The lily from its purity denotes peace, the net work from the intimate connections of its several parts denotes unity, and the pomegranates from the exuberance of its seed denote plenty. They were cast in the clay ground of the Jordan, between Succoth and Zarthan, where all the holy vessels of King Solomon's temple were cast, by Hiram Abiff, the widow's son of the tribe of Naphtali. They were further adorned with globals or balls, representing

globes celestial and terrestrial and signified the universality of Masonry.

The senior deacon now conducts the initiate through the pillars (between them) saying, "We will now advance three steps, stepping off with our left foot."

3 - 5 - 7 Steps in Masonry

The initiate is made to walk through each of these steps as they are explained to him:

These three steps allude to the first three degrees of Masonry: Entered Apprentice, Fellowcraft, and Master Mason. They also allude to the three principle officers of a lodge: Worshipful Master, Senior Warden, and Junior Warden.

The senior deacon now conducts the initiate, saying, "Brethren, we will now advance five steps, stepping off with the right foot." The senior deacon again steps in front and to the side of the initiate and says,

These five steps allude to the five steps in architecture. By order in architecture is meant a system of all the members, proportions, and ornaments of columns and pilasters; or, it is a regular arrangement of the projecting parts of a building, which, united with those of a column, form a beautiful, perfect, and complete whole. From the first formation of society, order in architecture may be traced. When the rigor of seasons obliged men to contrive shelter from the inclemency of the weather, we learn they first planted trees on end and then laid others

across to support a covering. The bands that connected those trees at top and bottom are said to
have given rise to the idea of the base and capital
of pillars, and from this simple hint originally proceeded the more improved art of architecture. The
five orders are thus classed: the Tuscan, Doric,
Ionic, Corinthian, and Composite. The ancient and
original orders of architecture revered by Masons
are no more than three: the Doric, Ionic, and
Corinthian, which were invented by the Greeks.
To these the Romans have added two: the Tuscan,
which they made plainer than the Doric; and the
Composite, which was more ornamental, if not
more beautiful, than the Corinthian. The first three
orders alone, however, show invention and particular character, and essentially differ from each
other; the two others have nothing but what is bor-
rowed, and differ only accidentally; the Tuscan is
the Corinthian enriched with the Ionic. To the
Greeks, therefore, and not to the Romans, are we
indebted for what is great, judicious, and distinct
in architecture. They also allude to the five senses
of human nature: hearing, seeing, feeling, smell-
ing, and tasting. The first three are most revered
by Masons, because by hearing we hear the word;
by seeing we perceive the sign; and by feeling we
receive the grip, whereby we may know one brother
from another, in the dark as well as in the light.

The senior deacon then states to the initiate,

Brethren, we will now advance seven steps,
stepping off with our left foot. These seven steps

allude to the seven liberal arts and sciences, which are grammar, rhetoric, logic, arithmetic, geometry, music, and astronomy. The fifth, geometry, is most revered by Masons. Geometry treats of the powers and properties of magnitudes in general, where length, breadth, and thickness are considered, from a point to a line, from a line to a superficies, and from a superficies to a solid. The point is a dimensionless figure, or an indivisible part of space. A line is a point continued, and a figure of one capacity; namely, length. A superficies is a figure of two dimensions; namely, length and breadth. A solid is a figure of three dimensions; namely, length, breadth, and thickness. By this science the architect is enabled to construct his plans and execute his designs; the general to arrange his soldiers; the geographer to give us the dimensions of the world and all things therein contained, to delineate the extent of seas, and to specify the divisions of empires, kingdoms, and provinces. By it, also, the astronomer is enabled to make his observations and to fix the duration of time and seasons, years and cycles. In fine, geometry is the foundation of architecture and the root of mathematics.[1]

But God's Word says,

As ye have therefore received Christ Jesus the Lord, so walk ye in him: rooted and built up in him, and stablished in the faith, as ye have been taught, abounding with thanksgiving. Beware lest any man spoil you through philosophy and vain deceit, after the tradition of men, after the rudiments of the world, and not after Christ. For in him dwelleth all the fulness of the Godhead bodily. And ye are complete in him, which is the head of all principality and power.

(Colossians 2:6–10)

If ye then be risen with Christ, seek those things which are above, where Christ sitteth on the right hand of God. Set your affection on things above, not on things on the earth. For ye are dead, and your life is hid with Christ in God. (Colossians 3:1–3)

---

[1]*Maryland Masonic Manual.*

Six

Excerpts from the Third Degree

❧

I n covering the ritual in Freemasonry known as the "Master Mason degree," first to be considered is the section dealing with eternal life.

Death, Burial, and Resurrection

Part one of the ritual deals with the beginning of the degree up to the obligation. Part two continues following the obligation up to the Worshipful Master's instruction to the initiate—getting dressed and returning to the lodge room.

The third section deals with raising the candidate from the "dead," who has already received his second degree, to represent a character by the name of Hiram Abiff, a slain workman of King Solomon's temple in Jerusalem.

First, it must be established that nowhere in Scripture will one find the death of Hiram Abiff. The books of 1 Kings or 2 Chronicles can be read with no mention of his death being recorded.

Hence, Freemasonry had to fabricate a story to suit its pagan ritual and purposes. The initiate is told that this part of the Master Mason degree is a legend. This story is so convincing that it is accepted as a true fact by the initiate.

The initiate is to represent an alleged biblical character in a legendary ritual of death and resurrection. Hiram Abiff, supposedly a workman in brass and other metals at King Solomon's temple, is presented in Masonic ritual as having been slain by three Fellowcrafters desiring the secrets of a Master Mason.

The initiate, after being met by three ruffians and literally shaken and pushed around, representing Hiram Abiff, is symbolically slain, mutilated, and buried at the base of an acacia tree.

After diligent "searching," the body of the initiate (Hiram Abiff) is found by Fellowcrafters of the second degree.

Hiram Abiff supposedly was in possession of a secret password, known as the Grand Masonic word. Since his death, it could not be given unless Hiram Abiff, Hiram of Tyre, and King Solomon were all present and agreed. So a substitute word was used by King Solomon, represented by the Worshipful Master of the lodge, who, in Masonic rite, raises the initiate's body from the "dead" and gives it "eternal life."

Hiram Abiff, whom the initiate represents, allegedly came from Phoenicia, a pagan country that worshipped Baal, the sun god. King Solomon, represented by the

Worshipful Master of the lodge, fell into idol worship. The ceremony uses Bible characters and verses for some of the story, but adds myth to suit the rite.

After a prayer and other rituals, the initiate is raised upon the five points of fellowship. When the Master raises the initiate, he whispers in his ear the Grand Masonic word ("*Mah-Hah-Bone*"). The Master then says to the newly raised brother,

> Brother ———, you have now been raised to the sublime degree of Master Mason, and the word that I have just communicated is the Grand Masonic word. You were raised by the strong grip of a Master Mason, or the lion's paw, and upon the five points of fellowship, which are....

The Master then takes the brother's hand and shows him how to do this grip, and says to the brother, "Follow me. Foot to foot, knee to knee, breast to breast, hand to back, and cheek to cheek or mouth to ear, give me the word." If the brother forgot the word, the Master in this position gives it to him again. The position of giving the Grand Masonic word (five points of fellowship) is the only way it can be given. The Master then steps back from the brother and explains the five points of fellowship:

> Foot to foot, so that you will be ever ready to go on foot or out of your way to assist and serve a worthy brother. Knee to knee, so that you will remember a brother's welfare, as well as your own. Breast to breast, so that you will keep the secrets

of a brother Master Mason as inviolable in your breast as they were in his before being communicated. Hand to back, so that you will be ever ready to stretch forth your hand to assist and save a fallen brother. Cheek to cheek, or mouth to ear, so that you will whisper good counsel in the ear of a brother in a most friendly manner, remind him of his error, and aid him in a reformation.

He that believeth on the Son hath everlasting life: and he that believeth not the Son shall not see life; but the wrath of God abideth on him. (John 3:36)

Know ye not that, as many of us as were baptized into Jesus Christ were baptized into his death? Therefore we are buried with him by baptism into death: that like as Christ was raised up from the dead by the glory of the Father, even so we also should walk in newness of life. (Romans 6:3–4)

Therefore if any man be in Christ, he is a new creature: old things are passed away; behold, all things are become new. (2 Corinthians 5:17)

It is important to remember that the Jewish and Muslim Masonic lodges are initiating candidates using the same ritual just described. They would certainly not submit to this ceremony of resurrection if there was any ritual semblance of God's Son, Jesus Christ, mentioned or implied.

For even hereunto were ye called: because Christ also suffered for us, leaving us an example, that ye should follow his steps. (1 Peter 2:21)

It is not expedient to examine the entire list of rituals that take place in the lectures and explanations of this degree. However, it can be documented that what is done is not Christian. The meanings given are clear to a candidate participating in the rite. This should be enough to expose this counterfeit of God's Word. What one may not realize is that there is an invisible meaning behind what the initiate has gone through:

> The mode and steps of the rituals were chosen for a particular reason, regardless of what interpretation Freemasonry puts into them. The procedure of the grave and steps taken to raise the man were chosen for a specific reason never given to the candidate. Every single point in the "Legend of Osiris," the Sun God, has its literal counterpart in the mysteries of Masonry in relation to the supposed death, burial, and pretended raising of Hiram Abiff in the third degree. Even the manner of raising Hiram Abiff in the Masonic lodge, the position of the Worshipful Master over the prostrate candidate, and the means adopted for his supposed restoration to life—the lion's paw—were actually represented among the hieroglyphics of ancient Egypt and have all been borrowed from the same source. The whole story of the murder of Hiram Abiff is a profane falsehood. Hiram Abiff was never murdered. Solomon never gave any such sign or uttered any such words! The whole story is false! Both the grand hailing sign of distress and the accompanying words are a profane mockery and an insult to God.[1]

The Book of Constitutions Guarded by Tyler's Sword

The explanation of the *Book of Constitutions Guarded by Tyler's Sword* given to the Masonic candidate is found in the *Masonic Manual*:

> The Book of Constitutions, guarded by Tyler's Sword, reminds us that we should be ever watchful and guarded in our words and actions, particularly when before the enemies of Masonry, ever bearing in remembrance those truly Masonic virtues, silence and circumspection.

The Book of Constitutions contains all the rules and regulations establishing the format of the institution. It was written by Rev. James Anderson in 1723 in England.

There is only one of two ways this explanation can be taken: first, it means the Mason should be silent and watchful when before the enemies of Masonry, regarding what is actually written in the *Book of Constitutions*; or, second, it refers to being silent and watchful about the secrets or mysteries conveyed to the candidate in his rituals, which he also was obligated upon a Bible and a death penalty not to reveal.

The second meaning is supported by all of the Order except a few uninformed Masons. The Mason is warned that the mysteries or secrets he has been taught and charged with are to be guarded, particularly when before the enemies of Masonry. The only enemies are Christians.

For the Christian, such teachings are limited exclusively to the reading and strict following of God's Word, from Genesis to Revelation. Christians are not to allow themselves to be taught anything in the area of spiritual or moral truths that are from doctrinal systems that can be proved to be contrary to God's Word. Freemasonry accepts into its portals almost every religious teaching in the world. Since Christianity is completely contrary to all of Masonic doctrine, it stands to reason that the only enemy of Masonry would be Jesus Christ and His disciples—the church of Jesus Christ.

In the book of Acts, Peter and John were preaching in the temple. The priests warned them several times not to preach or teach in the name of Jesus Christ. The priests even had them flogged. But because they were ordained by God and filled with the Spirit, they spoke out, unconcerned with the consequences because of their love for and loyalty to Christ. Most of the people they preached to were enemies of Christ or those who had never heard the salvation message. There was nothing to hide in their teachings. Why does Freemasonry warn its members to keep the rituals secret? It is because their rituals do not proceed from God, but instead are pagan in nature. About four hundred high Masons in this country will know exactly what is meant here.

A Mason in a lodge room may not always realize that the designs, setups, and movements are based on worship of the sun, and generative forces of nature, as practiced by the sex cults in ancient times. God's Word contains the true precepts believers are to follow, one example of which is Colossians 3:16:

> *Let the word of Christ dwell in you richly in all wisdom;
> teaching and admonishing one another in psalms and
> hymns and spiritual songs, singing with grace in your
> hearts to the Lord.*

> *But grow in grace, and in the knowledge of our Lord
> and Saviour, Jesus Christ. To him be glory both now
> and for ever. Amen.* (2 Peter 3:18)

God's Word furnishes light, which is found in John
8:12: "*Then spake Jesus again unto them, saying, I am the
light of the world; he that followeth me shall not walk in darkness, but shall have the light of life.*"

God's Word is a probing instrument in the Christian's
life. This is revealed in Hebrews 4:12:

> *For the word of God is quick, and powerful, and
> sharper than any twoedged sword, piercing even to the
> dividing asunder of soul and spirit, and of the joints and
> marrow, and is a discerner of the thoughts and intents
> of the heart.*

The Word of God purifies the Christian's life, as we
see in John 17:17: "*Sanctify them through thy truth: thy
word is truth.*"

The Bible relates human experiences as a warning, as
we discover in 1 Corinthians 10:11: "*Now all these things
happened unto them for ensamples: and they are written for
our admonition, upon whom the ends of the world are come.*"

The Bible declares itself to be the Christian's guide:

> *For whatsoever things were written aforetime were
> written for our learning, that we through patience and*

comfort of the scriptures might have hope. Now the God
of patience and consolation grant you to be likeminded
one toward another according to Christ Jesus.

(Romans 15:4–5)

Masonic lectures are teachings in which each candidate must participate in order to proceed to higher degrees. It is through these lectures that the majority of the doctrines or beliefs are laid out for the candidate, instructing him in a moral life. All of the doctrines given the candidate in his third degree pertain to life and death, as well as life after death. It is the whole purpose of the third degree, or Master Mason's degree, to impress on the mind of the Mason his new character that he is supposed to imitate in life. The Master Mason in the third degree is told he is to represent Hiram Abiff. The new life the Mason is to represent in his everyday conduct is contrary to life in Christ.

The Sword and the All-Seeing Eye

In the lecture of the third degree, the Mason is told about the sword pointing to the naked heart, and the all-seeing eye. He is told that the sword demonstrates that justice will sooner or later overtake him. Although his thoughts, words, and actions may be hidden from the eyes of man, the all-seeing eye, which the sun, moon, and stars obey, pervades the innermost recesses of the human heart and will reward the Mason according to his merits.

Albert Mackey, in *Encyclopedia of Freemasonry* (page 781), states that the sword pointing to the heart is to indicate that punishment would duly follow violation of the Mason's obligation. The all-seeing eye is a symbol of god manifested in omnipresence. It is interesting to note that Mackey, in his explanation of the all-seeing eye, makes reference to the book of Psalms, as giving reference to the eye of the Lord. Mackey also mentions in his book "that on the same principle, the Egyptians represented Osiris, their chief deity, by the symbol of an open eye, and placed hieroglyphics of it in all of their temples."

Never did any prophet in the Old Testament look at God as some giant eye overseeing His creation. The prophets many times had personal encounters with the living God. In the New Testament, this personal God has been revealed in and through the person of Jesus Christ, who now and forever possesses an immortal glorified body.

The Mason is told this all-seeing eye pervades the innermost recesses of the human heart. Hebrews 4:12 explains that it is the written Word that pervades the innermost recesses of the human heart. It is the living Word, Jesus Christ, and the written Word, the Bible, that shall judge all people.

Masonry says the all-seeing eye, which represents any deity, will, after searching the human heart, reward man according to his merits. But Christians know it is the person of Jesus Christ who will reward men according to their faith. Christians receive rewards for faithfulness. Works done by those who are not born-again Christians are *as filthy rags* (Isaiah 64:6).

The heart is deceitful above all things, and desperately wicked: who can know it? (Jeremiah 17:9)

But we are all as an unclean thing, and all our righteousnesses are as filthy rags; and we all do fade as a leaf; and our iniquities, like the wind, have taken us away. (Isaiah 64:6)

For we are his workmanship, created in Christ Jesus unto good works, which God hath before ordained that we should walk in them. (Ephesians 2:10)

And I saw the dead, small and great, stand before God; and the books were opened: and another book was opened, which is the book of life: and the dead were judged out of those things which were written in the books, according to their works. And the sea gave up the dead which were in it; and death and hell delivered up the dead which were in them: and they were judged every man according to their works. And death and hell were cast into the lake of fire. This is the second death. And whosoever was not found written in the book of life was cast into the lake of fire. (Revelation 20:12-15)

Charge—Third Degree

Let us look briefly at the charge given to an initiate who has just been made a Master Mason, or raised to the third degree of Masonry. Each paragraph of the charge will be examined against Scripture. The first paragraph of the charge is given as the initiate stands behind an altar with Bible open and officers and members present. It states,

Brother, your zeal for the institution of Masonry, the progress you have made in the mystery, and your conformity to our regulations have pointed you out as a proper object of our favor and esteem. You are now bound by duty, honor, and gratitude to be faithful to your trust; to support the dignity of your character on every occasion; and to enforce, by precept and example, obedience to the tenets of the Fraternity.

One cannot help but notice that Masonry is making it very clear that this third degree charge binds one by duty, gratitude, and honor to uphold what it teaches on every occasion.

Philippians 2:5 says, *"Let this mind be in you, which was also in Christ Jesus."*

The Bible also says in Romans 12:2,

And be not conformed to this world: but be ye transformed by the renewing of your mind, that ye may prove what is that good, and acceptable, and perfect, will of God.

The next paragraph of this charge reads, "In the character of a Master Mason you are authorized to correct the errors and irregularities of your uninformed brethren, and to guard them against a breach of fidelity." Visualize being commissioned as a Christian to correct errors and irregularities according to Masonic philosophy and doctrines. How can a Mason correct errors of another when he is not following the Truth?

Masonry qualifies a man to judge other men on the basis of its own teachings, not God's. The charge says

Excerpts from the Third Degree ✤

that the Mason is to guard his brothers in the lodge against a breach of fidelity or trust. These charges are not to be taken lightly; otherwise, there would not be such a thing as Masonic trials.

The next paragraph states,

> To preserve the reputation of the Fraternity unsullied must be your constant care; and for this purpose it is your province to recommend to your inferiors, obedience and submission; to your equals, courtesy and affability; to your superiors, kindness and condescension.

Second Corinthians 4:11 states, *"For we which live are alway delivered unto death for Jesus' sake, that the life also of Jesus might be made manifest in our mortal flesh."* Philippians 1:21 states, *"For to me to live is Christ, and to die is gain."* Luke 10:27 states, *"Thou shalt love the Lord thy God with all thy heart, and with all thy soul, and with all thy strength, and with all thy mind; and thy neighbour as thyself."* John 5:23 states, *"All men should honour the Son, even as they honour the Father. He that honoureth not the Son honoureth not the Father which hath sent him."*

Is it possible to preserve the reputation of Freemasonry with constant care and stay true to the above Scriptures? If we are to be true to God's Word and the Lord Jesus Christ, a Christian cannot preserve the reputation of a cult.

The next paragraph in this charge states,

> Universal benevolence you are always to incul-cate, and by the regularity of your own behavior,

afford the best example for the conduct of others less informed. The ancient landmarks of the institution, entrusted to your care, you are carefully to preserve; and never suffer them to be infringed, or countenance a deviation from the established usages and customs of the Fraternity. Your virtue, honor, and reputation are concerned in supporting with dignity the character you now bear.

The Mason who is a Christian is to uphold the landmarks and customs of Freemasonry, whose landmarks and customs are not biblical.

The nineteenth, twentieth, twenty-first, twenty-second, and twenty-third landmarks of Freemasonry say, in brief, that every Mason must believe in the existence of God as the Grand Artificer of the Universe; that he must believe in a resurrection to a future life; that a book of the law must be on the altar; that all men meet in the lodge room on an equal basis; and that since Freemasonry is a secret society, its practices cannot be divulged.

Masonry refers to God as the Grand Artificer of the Universe, a term acceptable by all religions except Christianity. In John 1:2-3, the person given credit for the creation of the universe is Jesus Christ.

The belief in a resurrection to a future life as portrayed by Masonry in the third degree is not Christ-centered.

Also, a book of the law must be on the altar—not the Bible, but just a book of any law. This allows Freemasonry to initiate men from nearly all religions because every religion has a book of "law."

In the lodge room, all men meet together on one common level, but this type of fellowship and union should be avoided by the Christian. In church we meet together in the name of Jesus Christ. In Masonry, this is not possible.

Masonry reminds the Mason that he is a member of a secret society, something that should never be named among Christians. Christians are children of light. Secrecy produces darkness.

The last paragraph states,

> Let no motive, therefore, make you swerve from your duty, violate your vows, or betray your trust; but be true and faithful, and imitate the example of that celebrated artist whom you have this evening represented. Thus you will render yourself deserving of the honor which we have conferred, and merit the confidence that we have reposed.

The celebrated artist (Hiram Abiff) he is to represent is completely contrary in person and life to the Person whom Christians represent.

Pot of Incense

This will be a brief look at the explanation given in the lectures for the Pot of Incense. It reads,

> [It] is an emblem of a pure heart, which is always an acceptable sacrifice to the Deity; and as this glows with fervent heat, so should our hearts continually glow with gratitude to the great and

beneficent Author of our existence for the manifold blessings and comforts we enjoy.

The Bible says in Jeremiah 17:9, *"The heart is deceitful above all things, and desperately wicked: who can know it?"* It also says in Matthew 22:37–38, *"Thou shalt love the Lord thy God with all thy heart, and with all thy soul, and with all thy mind. This is the first and great commandment."*

Until a person has accepted Jesus Christ as Savior and Lord, his heart is as Jeremiah said: evil. But after a person has been born again, he can then love God as commanded in these verses in Matthew. Only after salvation through Christ is the heart clothed with righteousness, and never before.

The Anchor and the Ark

According to the *Maryland Masonic Manual*, the anchor and the ark

> are emblems of a well-grounded hope and a well-spent life. They are emblematic of that Divine Ark which safely wafts us over this tempestuous sea of troubles, and that Anchor which shall safely moor us in a peaceful harbor, where the wicked shall cease from troubling, and the weary shall find rest.

In contrast to this, the Bible says in Isaiah 26:3, *"Thou wilt keep him in perfect peace, whose mind is stayed on thee: because he trusteth in thee."* The Christian's inner peace should come from meditating on Christ. Our hope is to be in the Lord, as indicated in 1 Peter 1:3:

Blessed be the God and Father of our Lord Jesus Christ, which according to his abundant mercy hath begotten us again unto a lively hope by the resurrection of Jesus Christ from the dead.

The Forty-seventh Problem of Euclid

According to the *Maryland Masonic Manual*, the Forty-seventh Problem of Euclid

> was an invention of our ancient friend and brother, the great Pythagoras, who, in his travels through Asia, Africa, and Europe, was initiated into several orders of Priesthood and raised to the sublime degree of Master Mason. This wise philosopher enriched his mind abundantly in a general knowledge of things and more especially in Geometry or Masonry. On this subject he drew out many problems and theorems, and among the most distinguished, he erected this, which in the joy of his heart he called "Eureka!" signifying in the Grecian language *"I have found it,"* and upon the discovery of which, he is said to have sacrificed a hecatomb. It teaches Masons to be general lovers of the arts and sciences.

To such a concept, the Word of God gives this warning found in Colossians 2:8: *"Beware lest any man spoil you through philosophy and vain deceit, after the tradition of men, after the rudiments of the world, and not after Christ."*

The Hour Glass

According to the *Maryland Masonic Manual*, the Hour Glass

is an emblem of human life. Behold, how swiftly
the sands run, and how rapidly our lives are drawing to a close! We cannot without astonishment
behold the little particles that are contained in this
machine; how they pass away almost impercepti-
bly; and yet, to our surprise, in the short space of
an hour they are all exhausted. Thus wastes man!
Today, he puts forth the tender leaves of hope;
tomorrow, blossoms, and bears his blushing honors
thick upon him: the next day comes a frost, which
nips the shoot, and when he thinks his greatness is
still aspiring, he falls, like autumn leaves, to enrich
our mother earth.

To this explanation of time and what it accomplishes,
the Bible offers this alternative description of life, found
in Philippians 1:6: *"Being confident of this very thing, that
he which hath begun a good work in you will perform it until
the day of Jesus Christ."*

The Scythe

According to the *Maryland Masonic Manual*, the
Scythe

is an emblem of time that cuts the brittle thread
of life and launches us into eternity. Behold, what
havoc the scythe of time makes among the human
race! If by chance we should escape the numerous
evils incident to childhood and youth, and with
health and vigor arrive at the years of manhood;
yet withal, we must soon be cut down by the
all-devouring scythe of time, and be gathered into

the land where our fathers have gone before us. The setting maul, the instrument by which our Grand Master Hiram Abiff was slain, teaches us...which will erelong take our life. The spade that opened his grave will sooner or later open ours, and the grave that carried his remains will erelong carry ours. Thus we close the explanation of the emblems upon the solemn thought of death, which without revelation is dark and gloomy. But by the strong grip of a Master Mason (or lion's paw) and by faith in the merits of the Lion of the tribe of Judah, we are strengthened with confidence and composure to look forward to the grave, and to doubt not; but in the glorious morn of the resurrection, our bodies will be raised and become as immortal as our souls. By the sprig of acacia buried at the head of the grave that bears the nearest affinity to that supreme intelligence that pervades nature, we are taught that we shall never, never, never die.

At this point, the Worshipful Master raps the lodge up (three raps) and then continues.

Then, my brethren, let us imitate our Grand Master Hiram Abiff in his virtuous and amiable conduct, in his unfeigned piety to God, in his inflexible fidelity to his trust; that we may welcome the grim tyrant death, and receive him as a kind messenger sent from our Supreme Grand Master to translate us from this imperfect to that all perfect, glorious, and celestial lodge above, where the Supreme Architect of the Universe (S.A.O.T.U.) presides.

All officers and members bow toward the East. The Master raps the lodge down (one rap). Also explained to the brother in the third degree lecture is what he is to do in times of peril or danger. He is instructed (if he can be seen) to throw up both arms over his head and let them fall by three distinct motions. This is the grand hailing sign or sign of distress; it should never be given except in a lodge for instruction or if his life is in danger. If a Mason sees this sign, he is to flee to his rescue if there is more probability of saving the brother's life than of losing his own.

At times when this sign cannot be seen, such as in the dark, a spoken signal is substituted: "*O Lord, my God, is there no help for the widow's son?*" A Mason hearing these words would be equally bound to flee to the brother's rescue if there were more probability of saving his brother's life than of losing his own.

The Bible paints quite a different picture of the end of life, whether by death or by the rapture of the church, and how we are to regard death. It says in 1 Corinthians 15:51–58,

> Behold, I show you a mystery; we shall not all sleep, but we shall all be changed, in a moment, in the twinkling of an eye, at the last trump: for the trumpet shall sound, and the dead shall be raised incorruptible, and we shall be changed. For this corruptible must put on incorruption, and this mortal must put on immortality. So when this corruptible shall have put on incorruption, and this mortal shall have put on immortality, then shall be brought to pass the saying that is written, Death is swallowed up in victory. O death, where is thy sting?

O grave, where is thy victory? The sting of death is sin; and the strength of sin is the law. But thanks be to God, which giveth us the victory through our Lord Jesus Christ. Therefore, my beloved brethren, be ye stedfast, unmoveable, always abounding in the work of the Lord, forasmuch as ye know that your labour is not in vain in the Lord.

---

[1]Rev. Charles Finney, *The Character, Claims, and Practical Workings of Freemasonry* (Chicago: Ezra A. Cook).

Seven

Masonic Questions and Answers

hat follows are only a few of the many questions and answers found in the first three degrees of Masonry.

These answers must be memorized and perfectly presented orally before the brother can pass on to his next degree. Since all three degrees follow the same basic pattern of questions, with sometimes only slightly different answers, it would be pointless to list the approximately 144 questions and answers one must memorize.

First Degree

Question: Are you a Mason?
Answer: I am.

Q: What makes you a Mason?
A: My obligation.

Q: How do I know you to be a Mason?
A: By certain signs and tokens.

Q: What are signs?
A: Right angles, horizontals, and perpendiculars.

Q: What are tokens?
A: Certain grips whereby one brother may know another in the dark, as well as in the light.

Q: Where were you made a Mason?
A: In a legally constituted lodge of ancient free and accepted Masons.

Q: How were you prepared?
A: By being divested of all minerals and metals, neither naked nor clothed, barefoot nor shod, hoodwinked, with a cable tow about my neck, in which condition I was led to a door.

Q: Being hoodwinked, how did you know it was a door?
A: By first meeting with resistance, afterwards gaining admission.

Q: How did you gain admission?
A: By giving three distinct knocks from without, which were answered by a like number from within, with the question, Who comes here?

Q: Your answer?
A: (Name), a poor blind candidate, who desires to be brought from darkness to light, and receive a part of the rights and benefits of this right worshipful Lodge, erected to God, and dedicated to the Holy Saints John.

Q: What was then asked your conductor?
A: Was I duly and truly prepared, worthy, and well qualified?

Q: His answer?
A: He is. (Answer given by the conductor.)

Q: What was then asked you?
A: By what further right I expected to gain admission.

Q: Your answer?
A: By that of being a man, freeborn, of good report, and well recommended.

Q: What was then told you?
A: To wait as the Worshipful Master was informed of my request.

The rest of the many questions and answers follow the ritual as the degree progresses to the end.

Second Degree

In this degree, we will cover only some of the questions from the point of entrance into the lodge room, since they basically follow the first degree pattern.

Q: Upon your admission into the lodge, how were you received?
A: Upon the angle of a square piercing my naked right breast, which was to teach me that the square of truth and virtue should be the rule and guide of my conduct in all my future transactions with mankind.

Q: Where were you then conducted?
A: Twice around the lodge, where the same questions were asked and like answers given as at the door.

Q: Where were you then conducted?
A: To the senior warden in the West, who taught me how to approach the East in due masonic form, by taking two regular upright steps, my feet forming the angle of an oblong square, my body erect, facing the East.

Q: What were you then caused to do?
A: To be placed at the altar in due form to be made a Fellowcraft.

Q: Repeat the obligation?
A: (At this point, the entire class usually recites it.)

Q: In the dark and benighted condition in which we again find you, what is it you most desire?
A: Light.

Q: Did you receive it?
A: I did, by order of the Worshipful Master assisted by the brethren.

Q: Upon being brought to the light, what did you behold in this, more than in your preceding degree?
A: One point of the compass, elevated above the square, which is to teach me that, as yet, I had received light in Masonry, but partially.

Q: What did you next observe?

A: The Worshipful Master, approaching me from the East, under the due guard and sign of a Fellow-craft.

Q: Give me the due guard.
A: (The brother stands in the position of a Fellow-craft.)

Q: Give me the sign.
A: (The brother makes the sign of the penalty of the Fellowcraft degree.)

Q: What did you next observe?
A: The Worshipful Master a second time approaching me from the East, who gave me the passgrip and word of a Fellowcraft.

Q: Give it to me.
A: I did not so receive it, neither can I so impart it.

Q: How will you dispose of it?
A: I will syllablic it with you.

Q: Syllablic it and begin.
A: Nay, you begin.

Q: Nay, begin you.
A: Shib
  bo
  leth

Q: Pass on what is this?
A: The grip of a Fellowcraft.

Q: Has it a name?

A: It has.

Q: Will you give it to me?
A: I did not so receive it, neither can I so impart it.

Q: How will you dispose of it?
A: I will letter it with you.

Q: Letter it and begin.
A: Nay, you begin.

Q: Nay, begin you.
A: (candidate) A
   (instructor) J
   (c) C
   (i) H
   (c) I
   (i) N
   (c) Ja
   (i) chin

There are yet many questions and answers to this degree, following the degree to its conclusion. All of the steps (3-5-7) are gone over and memorized as to their meanings. Also, the meaning, in detail, of both pillars described in the ritual, as well as the battle scene, are to be memorized.

Third Degree

In the first degree we covered several of the questions and answers leading to the anteroom door. In the second degree, we covered the questions and answers from the door to the approach of the Worshipful Master at the altar. In this third degree, we will cover from that point at the altar to the conclusion.

Q: What were you then caused to do?
A: To arise and salute the junior and senior wardens.

Q: Where were you then conducted?
A: To the South, West, and East, where I gave the due guard and sign of a Master Mason.

Q: Give me the due guard.
A: (The brother stands up and makes the due guard of a Master Mason.)

Q: Give me the sign.
A: (Likewise, the brother stands up and makes the sign of the penalty of the third degree.)

Q: Where were you then conducted?
A: To the Worshipful Master in the East, who explained to me the working tools of a Master Mason.

Q: What are the working tools of a Master Mason?
A: All the implements of Masonry, indiscriminately, but more especially, the trowel.

Q: Where were you then conducted?
A: To the place from whence I came, there invested with what I had been divested of and returned to the lodge.

Q: Upon your return to the lodge, whom were you cause to represent?
A: Hiram Abiff.

Q: Who was Hiram Abiff?
A: First celebrated worker in brass and other metals.

Q: How were you raised?
A: By the strong grip of a Master Mason, or the lion's paw, and upon the five points of fellowship.

Q: What are the five points of fellowship?
A: Foot to foot, knee to knee, breast to breast, hand to back, and cheek to cheek or mouth to ear.

Q: Give me the Grand Masonic word.
A: I will as I have received it.

The instructor and brother being examined both stand up. They both take each other's right hand and grasp in the grip of a lion's paw. Then the brother steps off with his right foot, and the instructor puts his right foot next to and parallel to the brother's foot. The other four points of fellowship are then carried out the same way until they are both embraced. In this position the brother being examined then whispers in the ear of the instructor the Grand Masonic word, which is Mah-Hah-Bone.

Note

The Grand Masonic word once was Jehovah, but in 1779 was transferred to the "Royal Arch Degree" and Mah-Hah-Bone was substituted in its place by the manipulations of Ramsay, Dermott, and Dunckerley, three of the highest Masons at that time. The real spelling was actually Mah-Hah-Bonay, but through the years was corrupted and ended up Mah-Hah-Bone. Due to the great difficulty of undoing this corruption, it was decided to leave it in its corrupted form.

Deuteronomy 6:6–9 says,

> *And these words, which I command thee this day, shall be in thine heart: and thou shalt teach them diligently unto thy children, and shalt talk of them when thou sittest in thine house, and when thou walkest by the way, and when thou liest down, and when thou risest up. And thou shalt bind them for a sign upon thine hand, and they shall be as frontlets between thine eyes. And thou shalt write them upon the posts of thy house, and on thy gates.*

The questions and answers of the various degrees are contrary to the above scriptural command to meditate on God's Word. God does not want the Christian to meditate on a series of questions and answers that war against the Spirit of truth.

Eight

Cloak of Satan

❖

The cloak of satan covering Freemasonry blinds many to the true character of its meaning. *"Ye shall know them by their fruits"* (Matthew 7:16). There also are Bible verses and Christian symbols displayed in the lodge room. Most Christian symbols are limited to the Commandery or Knights Templar, though. In the third degree, many Bible verses explaining eternal life and immortality are used. However, never once is Jesus Christ projected as the person of eternal life. Never once is He announced as the Resurrection and the Life. However, New Testament Scriptures are used in the Masonic Bibles to point out the fact of eternal life.

Each degree of Masonry uses Bible verses to support the ritual. This does not necessarily mean that God gave to men the verse for the purpose for which it is being used in the lodge room. For example, Hosea 11:4 reads, *"I drew them with cords of a man, with bands of love."* This is outlined in the Masonic Bible as the cable tow, a six-foot blue cord wrapped around the candidate's neck as he is led blindfolded into the lodge room. This same cable tow is the measurement of the distance from shore that Freemasonry will bury the mutilated body of someone who reveals its secrets.

The meeting in the lodge room is supported in the Masonic Bibles with Matthew 18:20: *"For where two or three are gathered together in my name, there am I in the midst of them."* But a lodge meeting is not a gathering of believers for the purpose of glorifying God. In the Masonic Bible, verses are very deceptively misused.

There is biblical terminology used in the lodge room, such as Jacob's ladder, Holy Bible, almighty God, Jehovah, Savior, I Am that I Am, from darkness to light, ask and ye shall receive, seek and ye shall find, knock and it shall be opened unto you, and much more.

For an example, the phrase "ask, seek, and find" is taken from the Sermon on the Mount, Matthew 7:7. John 14:13 reads, *"And whatsoever ye shall ask in my name, that will I do, that the Father may be glorified in the Son."* John 15:16 reads, *"Ye have not chosen me, but I have chosen you, and ordained you, that ye should go and bring forth fruit, and that your fruit should remain: that whatsoever ye shall ask of the Father in my name, he may give it you."* In Matthew 6:33, Jesus says, *"But seek ye first the kingdom of God, and his righteousness; and all these things shall be added unto you."* In Revelation 3:20 Christ says to John, *"Behold, I stand at the door and knock: if any man hear my voice, and open the door, I will come in to him, and will sup with him, and he with me."*

Cloak of Satan 🌿

All asking, seeking, and knocking must be in the name of Jesus Christ, to the glory of the Father. Christ knocks for you to open up the door of your heart to Him to save you, and seeking the kingdom of God is only in and through Jesus Christ. What one is seeking in Freemasonry is a light into hidden things, secrets involving soul and spirit, not according to God's Word, but according to clever perversion of God's Word.

All through Masonry there is biblical terminology used contrary to God's Word. Remember what Paul said to Timothy in 2 Timothy 2:15? *"Study to show thyself approved unto God, a workman that needeth not to be ashamed, rightly dividing the word of truth."*

Then there are objects of worship, such as the Bible and various symbols. Is the Bible on the altar the Old and New Testaments? In some lodges, yes, but never on the Jewish Mason's altar or on the Muslim Mason's altar. This leaves the Bible in no better position than other writings of the other religions of the world.

Discussing the religious nature of Freemasonry, Dr. Romasseun, graduate of Bob Jones University, presents this case:

> For a Christian who has done even a minimal amount of reading in Masonic books to ask the question, "Is Freemasonry a false religion?" it is the same as asking "Is the Pope Catholic?"
>
> To properly answer the question, "Is Freemasonry a false religion?" let us begin by first establishing the fact that Masonry is a religion. The Lord Jesus

Christ said, *"In the mouth of two or three witnesses every word may be established"* (Matthew 18:16). In order to save space, there will be only four Masonic authorities quoted to prove that Masonry is a religion.

Albert Mackey, one of the most well-known Masonic authorities in *A Lexicon of Freemasonry* wrote (p. 402), "The religion, then Masonry, is pure theism."

Albert Pike, the most important of all American Masonic authorities in *Morals and Dogma* wrote (pp. 213–214), "Every Masonic lodge is a temple of religion, and its teachings are instructions in religion....This is the true religion revealed to the ancient patriarchs; which Masonry has taught for many centuries, and which it will continue to teach as long as time endures."

J. S. M. Ward, a Masonic authority who has written several important books on Masonry, in his book *Freemasonry: Its Aims and Ideals* (p. 185), wrote, "I consider Freemasonry is a sufficiently organized school of mysticism to be entitled to be called a religion." Ward continued on page 187, "Freemasonry...taught that each man can, by himself, work out his own conception of God, and thereby achieve salvation." It holds that there are many paths that lead to the throne of the all-loving Father that all start from a common source. Freemasonry believes, according to Ward, "that though these paths appear to branch off in various directions, yet they all reach the same ultimate goal, and that to some men, one path is better, and to others, another."

Frank C. Higgins, a high Mason, in *Ancient Freemasonry* wrote (p. 10), "It is true that Freemasonry is the parent of all religion."

These Masonic witnesses all agree in their doctrine that Masonry is, indeed, a religion. It is necessary to ascertain whether Masonry is a true religion or a false religion....

In an article entitled, "How to Recognize False Religion" (*Faith for the Family*, November–December, 1974), a prominent Christian leader wrote, "All false religions, however, have some things in common. Here are three simple tests by which any religion should be judged. First, what is its attitude toward the Bible? In the second place, any religious teaching should be tested by this question: What is its attitude toward Jesus Christ? Finally, in judging a religious system, we should ask, What is its attitude toward the blood of Jesus Christ?"

According to these three tests, Masonry is undoubtedly a false religion and manifests a satanic attitude toward the Bible, the deity of Jesus Christ, and the blood atonement of our Lord and Savior Jesus Christ. In order to establish the above charge, let us keep in mind the words of our Lord Jesus Christ, who said, *"In the mouth of two or three witnesses every word may be established"* (Matthew 18:16). Please consider now the testimonies of Masonic authorities, which reveal Masonry's satanic attitude toward the Bible, the deity of Jesus Christ, and the vicarious atonement for the sins of mankind by the shedding of Christ's blood on the cross.

Joseph Fort Newton, a famous Masonic authority and writer, in an article entitled "The Bible and Masonry" (which appears in the front of the Masonic Bible), wrote, "The Bible, so rich in symbolism, is itself a symbol....Thus, by the very honor that Masonry pays to the Bible, it teaches us to revere every book of faith in which men find help for today and hope for tomorrow, joining hands with the man of Islam as he takes oath on the Koran, and with the Hindu as he makes covenant with God upon the book that he loves best."

Albert Pike, in *Morals and Dogma,* wrote (p. 718), "Masonry propagates no creed except its own most simple and sublime one; that universal religion, taught by nature and reason."

One who is truly born again can see from the above statement that Masonry totally rejects the doctrine of an infallible, God-breathed, inerrant Bible.

According to the second test, Masonry is a false religion because it totally rejects the crucial doctrine of the deity of the Lord Jesus Christ.

J. D. Buck, M.D., another Masonic writer of importance, in his book *Symbolism or Mystic Masonry* wrote (p. 57), "In the early church, as in the secret doctrine, there was not one Christ for the world, but a potential Christ in every man. Theologians first made a fetish of the Impersonal

Omnipresent Divinity; and then tore the Christos from the hearts of all humanity in order to deify Jesus; that they might have a god-man peculiarly their own."

Dr. R. Swinburne Clymer, M.D., who is recognized as a high Mason, in his book *The Mysticism of Masonry* wrote (p. 47), " In deifying Jesus, the whole humanity is bereft of Christos as an eternal potency within every human soul, a latent (embryonic) Christ in every man. In thus deifying one man, they have orphaned the whole of humanity." He added that at the same time, they have built "a false and destructive scheme of salvation." Few candidates may be aware that Hiram, whom they have represented and personified, is ideally and precisely the same as Jesus.

One would have to look far and wide anywhere in the writings of false teachers to find statements more blasphemous than these about the person of Jesus Christ.

According to the third test, Masonry is a false religion because it dogmatically rejects the doctrine of salvation from the penalty of sin by faith in the vicarious atonement of Christ's shed blood on the cross.

Please consider carefully what the following Masonic witnesses have written regarding the vicarious atonement of Christ.

J. D. Buck, M.D., in *Symbolism or Mystic Masonry* wrote (p. 57), "Every soul must work out its own salvation...salvation by faith and the vicarious atonement were not taught as now interpreted, by Jesus, nor are these doctrines taught in the esoteric scriptures. They are later and ignorant perversions of the original doctrines."

Thomas Milton Steward, another Masonic author, in his book *Symbolic Teaching or Masonry and Its Message*, to support his doctrine, quoted favorably an apostate Episcopal minister who wrote (p. 177), "Did Jesus Himself conceive of Himself as a propitiatory sacrifice, and of His work as an expiation? The only answer possible is, clearly He did not....He does not call Himself the world's priest, or the world's victim."

Salvation by faith and the vicarious atonement are not "ignorant perversions of the original doctrines," as Masonry teaches, but they are vital ingredients of the glorious Gospel of Christ, which is *"the power of God unto salvation to every one that believeth"* (Romans 1:16).

Therefore, Masonry fails all three tests. It manifests a satanic attitude toward the Bible, the deity of Christ, and the vicarious atonement. In addition to failing these tests, there is much more proof that Masonry is a false religion.

For instance, Henry C. Clausen, thirty-third degree, Sovereign Grand Commander of the Supreme Council thirty-third degree, Mother Council of the World, in the *New Age*, November 1970 (p. 4), regarding Masonry wrote, "It is dedication to bringing about the Fatherhood of God, the

Brotherhood of Man, and the making of better men in a better world."

The doctrine of the Fatherhood of God and the Brotherhood of Man is not found in the Bible, but it is a doctrine taught consistently by apostates. Also, the Bible makes it crystal clear that no organization—Masonry included—can make better men. Only God can do that.

According to a Masonic creed found in the Masonic Bible, Masonry teaches that "character determines destiny."

The teaching that character determines destiny is a false doctrine of the arch deceiver of souls. The Bible says, *"There is none that doeth good"* (Psalm 14:1), and *"For by grace are ye saved through faith: and that not of yourselves: it is the gift of God: not of works, lest any man should boast"* (Ephesians 2:8–9).

Masonry is anti-Christian in its teaching. For example, J. M. Ward in *Freemasonry: Its Aims and Ideals* wrote (p. 187), "I boldly aver that Freemasonry is a religion, yet in no way conflicts with any other religion, unless that religion holds that no one outside its portals can be saved." Ward, in this statement, reveals the fact that Masonry has no conflict with any apostate religion on the face of the earth, but he also reveals that Masonry is in conflict with biblical Christianity. The Bible says, *"Neither is there salvation in any other: for there is none other name under heaven given among men, whereby we must be saved"* (Acts 4:12). Jesus said, *"No man cometh unto the Father, but by me"* (John 14:6). The Bible is plain in its teaching that there is only one way to heaven, and that is Christ.

Dr. Bob Jones, III, president of Bob Jones University, in a letter dedicated to Mr. Thomas D. Resinger on June 30, 1974, wrote of Masonry, "It is a luciferian religion. We are fully aware of its diabolical origin and purpose. I believe that any born-again Christian, when the facts from the lips of the Masonic writers themselves are presented showing that Masonry is a religion and is the worship of satan, will immediately withdraw."

Christian college founders like Dr. Jack Hyles and Dr. Bob Gray have stated forcefully that they will not permit Masons on their college boards. Fundamental Christian leaders like Dr. Charles Woodbridge, Dr. G. Archer Weniger, and Dr. Marion Reynolds, president of the American Council of Christian Churches for five years, have stated that it is unscriptural for Masons to be on the board of Christian institutions.

The God and Father of the Lord Jesus Christ, the only true and living God, has clearly commanded Christians, *"Be ye not unequally yoked together with unbelievers"* (2 Corinthians 6:14); *"Swear not at all"* (Matthew 5:34); and *"Have no fellowship with the unfruitful works of darkness, but rather reprove them"* (Ephesians 5:11).

Charles Finney, the famed evangelist whom God used to bring revival to America in the 1830s, in his book on Freemasonry wrote (p. 115), "Surely if Masons really understood what Masonry is, as it is delineated in these books, no Christian Mason would think himself at liberty to remain another day a member of the fraternity. It is as plain as possible that a man knowing what it is, and embracing it in his heart, cannot be a Christian man. To say he can is to belie the very nature of Christianity."[1]

Albert Mackey made a statement in his book, *Jurisprudence of Freemasonry*, that seems to be the key to removing the cloak of satan from the cult of Freemasonry and letting its true character, beliefs, and aims stand for all to behold. In the midst of explaining the twenty-third landmark of Freemasonry, he made this statement:

> Now this form of secrecy is a form inherent in it, existing with it from its very foundation and secured to it by its ancient landmarks. If divested of its secret character, it would lose its identity, and would cease to be Freemasonry. Whatever objections may, therefore, be made to the institution, on account of its secrecy, and however much some unskilled brethren have been willing in times of trial for the sake of expediency to divest it of its secret character, it will be ever impossible to do so, even were the landmarks not standing before us as an insurmountable obstacle; because such change of its character would be social suicide, and the death of the Order would follow its legalized exposure. Freemasonry, as a secret association, has lived unchanged for centuries; as an open society, it would not last for as many years.

Lambskin

In the first degree, an initiate is handed the greatest gift he can receive as a Mason. According to the *Maryland Masonic Manual,*

> This Lambskin, or white leather apron, which is an emblem of innocence, and the badge of a Mason; more ancient than the Golden Fleece or Roman Eagle, more honorable than the Star or Garter, or any other order that could be conferred upon you at this or any future period, by King, Prince, Potentate, or any other person, except he be a Mason; and which I hope you will wear with plea-sure to yourself, and honor to the Fraternity.... You were presented with a Lambskin, or white leather apron, because the Lamb in all ages has been deemed an emblem of innocence. He, therefore, who wears the Lambskin as the "badge of a Mason" is continu-ally reminded of that purity of life and conduct which is so essentially necessary to his gaining admission into the Celestial Lodge above, where the Supreme Architect of the Universe presides.

Galatians 2:16 says,

> *Knowing that a man is not justified by the works of the law, but by the faith of Jesus Christ, even we have believed in Jesus Christ, that we might be justified by the faith of Christ, and not by the works of the law: for by the works of the law shall no flesh be justified.*

Masonry has used the lamb, which in the Old Testament has always been representative of the coming

Messiah, and is now representative of none other than Jesus Christ, the Lamb of God.

A Mason cannot attend lodge or funeral services without his apron on at all times. If the deceased is a Mason, he cannot have a Masonic service without his apron on his body. The Missouri Synod of the Lutheran Church prints through its Concordia Publishing House a small book denouncing the lamb-skin of Freemasonry. Here is a quote from Mr. W. L. Wilmhurst, Grand Registrar of West Yorkshire District, concerning Masonry's salvation:

> Our science in its universality limits our conception to no one exemplar. Take the nearest and most familiar to you, the one under whose aegis you were racially born, and who therefore may serve you best; for each is able to bring you to the center, though each may have his separate method. To the Jewish brother it says: Take the father of the faithful, and realize what being gathered to his bosom means. To the Christian brother, it points to him upon whose breast lay the beloved disciple. To the Hindu brother, it points to Krishna. To the Buddhist, it points to the Martreya of universal compassion. And to the Muslim it points to his Prophet, and the significance of being clothed in his mantle.[2]

Another Masonic author, J. S. M. Ward, quotes this poem of his:

> Bacchus died and rose again, on the golden Syrian Plain. Osiris rose from out of his grave and

thereby mankind did save; Adonis likewise did shed his blood, by the yellow Syrian flood; Zoroaster brought to birth Mirthra from his cave of earth. And we today in Christian lands, we with them, can join hands.[2]

What a mockery of God's Word this is, yet all Masonic authors and authorities run on the same satanic line of reasoning. God's Word says in 1 John 5:11–12, *"And this is the record, that God hath given to us eternal life, and this life is in his Son. He that hath the Son hath life; and he that hath not the Son of God hath not life."* John 3:16 says, *"For God so loved the world, that he gave his only begotten Son, that whosoever believeth in him should not perish, but have everlasting life."* God's perfect love is manifested in and through the person of Jesus Christ, who is the Way, the Truth, and the Life.

---

[1]Publisher for this article is The Projector, Milton, FL., or Gospel Projects Press, Milton, FL.

[2]Orthodox Presbyterian Church, *Christ or the Lodge* (Philadelphia: Great Commission Publications, 1942).

Nine

Opposition

❧

Great Men Who Opposed Masonry—
Prayers and Charges of Lodges

I want to share with you some great men who have renounced Freemasonry or have preached against it and all secret orders. The most spiritual and most trusted Christian leaders of the past and present have given their testimonies against secret orders and lodges, and have urged Christians who loved God to come out from among them and be separate. The great Moody Church in Chicago, founded by D. L. Moody, of which Dr. Harry A. Ironside was a longtime pastor, requires one to renounce lodges and secret orders to be a member of that church. Other pastors of that notable church were Drs. R. A. Torrey, Paul Rader, James M. Gray, and P. W. Philpot. The Cicero Bible Church, of which Rev. William McCarrell, longtime president of the Independent Fundamental Churches of America, has been pastor, has the same stand. Wheaton College at Wheaton, Illinois, has the same stand. Drs. Jonathan

Blanchard and Charles A. Blanchard, great presidents of Wheaton College, were widely known for their vigorous stand against lodges. Here is what D. L. Moody said about secret orders:

> I do not see how any Christian, most of all a Christian minister, can go into these secret lodges with unbelievers. They say they can have more influences for good; but I say they can have more influence for good by staying out of them, and then reproving their evil deeds. Abraham had more influence for good in Sodom than Lot had. If twenty-five Christians go into a secret lodge with fifty who are not Christians, the fifty can vote anything they please, and the twenty-five will be partakers of their sins. They are unequally yoked together with unbelievers. "But," says someone, "what do you say about these secret temperance orders?" I say the same thing. Do not evil that good may come. You can never reform anything by unequally yoking yourself with ungodly men. True reformers separate themselves from the world. "But," you say, "I had one of them in my church." So I had, but when I found out what it was, I cleaned it out like a cage of unclean birds. They drew in a lot of young men of the church in the name of temperance, and then they got up a dance and kept them out till after twelve at night. I was a partaker of their sins, because I let them get into the church; but they were cleaned out, and they never came back. This idea of promoting temperance by yoking oneself up that way with ungodly men is abominable. The most abominable

meeting I ever attended was a temperance meeting in England. It was full of secret societies, and there was no Christianity about it. I felt as though I had gotten into Sodom, and got out as soon as I could. A man rescued from intemperance by a society not working on gospel principles, gets filled with pride and boasts about reforming itself. Such a man is harder to save than a drunkard. "But Mr. Moody," some say, "if you talk that way, you will drive out all the members of secret societies out of your meetings and out of your churches." But what if I did? Better men will take their places. Give them the truth anyway, and if they would rather leave their churches than their lodges, the sooner they get out of the churches, the better. I would rather have ten members who are separated from the world than a thousand such members. Come out from the lodge. Better one with God, than a thousand without Him.

We must walk with God, and if only one or two go with us, it is all right. Do not let down the standards to suit men who love their secret lodges or have some darling sin they will not give up.

D. L. Moody was vigorous in his influence against secret orders. His great Christian Workers' Conference, with leading preachers and Bible teachers from England and America, led many a student and preacher to forsake secret orders.

Nazarene churches forbid members to join the lodges, as do the Mennonites and many branches of the Lutheran Church. The Christian Reformed denomination has denounced the lodge also, and forbids members to join the lodge.

The great evangelist, Charles Finney, who won some two hundred thousand souls to Christ and then founded Oberlin College, wrote a remarkable book entitled *The Character, Claims, and Practical Workings of Freemasonry.* This great preacher, soulwinner, educator, and writer gave proof so convincingly and plainly stated in such a Christian spirit, that it is overwhelming.

The book *Heresies Exposed,* compiled by William C. Irvine, editor of the *Indian Christian,* with introduction by Dr. Louis T. Talbot (longtime pastor of the Church of the Open Door and former president of the Bible Institute of Los Angeles), has gone through ten editions. Among the false cults exposed in this book is Freemasonry. There is an abundance of literature on the subject matter for earnest Christians. Notice the remarkable list of great Christian men and statesmen who have renounced the lodges and opposed them, particularly the Masons: John Wesley, Alexander Campbell, Daniel Webster, Wendell Phillips, Chief Justice Charles Marshall, Sharles Sumner, John Hancock, Horace Greeley, Joseph Cook, D. L. Moody, R. A. Torrey, Timothy Dwight, Charles Finney, J. H. Fairchild, Jonathan and Charles Blanchard (former presidents of Wheaton College), John Adams, John Quincy Adams, James Madison, Amos Well, Simon Peter Long, and James M. Gray. At one time Princeton Theological Seminary and other institutions offered courses in modern cults and false religions that included an exposure of the false teachings of fraternal orders.[1]

Prayers in a Lodge

In an article that was published in the *Maryland Master Mason* magazine in March 1973 (vol. 2), which is approved by the Grand Lodge of Maryland, we read the following:

> All prayers in Mason lodges should be directed to the one deity to whom all Masons refer as the Grand Architect of the Universe. He is addressed as Heavenly Father, Eternal God, or Almighty living God. Prayers in the lodges should be closed with expressions such as "in the most holy and precious name we pray," using no additional words that would be in conflict with the religious beliefs of those present at meetings. The brother who offers up the prayer does so for all members and visitors present, rather than just for himself.

In other words, a Mason may not close prayers in the name of the Lord Jesus Christ, as it would offend lodge brothers who are Jews, Muslims, Buddhists, and so on.

As the Worshipful Master of a Baltimore lodge in 1968, I was told by the Grand Secretary of Maryland, "If you want to worship Jesus Christ, go to your church; we worship the Supreme Architect of the Universe here." This Grand Lodge Secretary, who was a very influential member of long standing in the Grand Lodge of Maryland, did not make this statement in a very friendly attitude. He was very upset by my question regarding the worship of God. But he became very much more distraught when I replied to his answer, "You are telling me to go to church to worship Christ, because in the lodge room you worship the Grand Architect of the Universe. What is the difference in the light of John 1:3, which reads, '*All things were made by him; and without him was not any thing made that was made*'? This passage, of course, is speaking of Christ Jesus. This means that Christ is coequal with the Father and Spirit in creation, and yet you separate the Godhead, as if Christ didn't exist. How can you do this?"

Bill Gothard, in his book on *Basic Youth Conflicts*, made a statement on prerequisites for prayer to God the Father. The first was the following:

> The petitioner must be in right standing with the one he is petitioning. Those who appeal to God must be in right standing with Him. Only those who have put their faith and trust in the Lord Jesus Christ are the sons of God. Only they have the right to address God as their heavenly Father (Matthew 7:21).

Freemasonry denies such a prerequisite for prayer. Some may say, "Why, our lodge Chaplain prays in the name of the Lord Jesus Christ and no one objects, so what's the problem?"

The problem of prayers in the lodge room is just this: the Grand Lodge of the state can order the Worshipful Master of that lodge to cease closing his prayers in Christ's name or be closed down as a lodge. The Grand Master has this authority.

The following is a statement written by a Presbyterian minister, James Anderson, one of the two founders of

Freemasonry. It was published in the first *Book of Constitutions* in 1723:

> A Mason is obliged by his Tensure, to obey the Moral Law, and if he rightly understands the Art, he will never be a stupid atheist nor an irreligious libertine. But though in ancient times, Masons were charged in every country to be of the religion of that country or nation, whatever it was, yet 'tis now thought more expedient only to oblige them to that religion in which all men agree, leaving their particular opinions to themselves, that is, to be good men and true, or men of honor and honesty, by whatsoever denominations or persuasions they may be distinguished.

Whether it be Anderson in 1723 or Pike and Mackey in 1870 or the Grand Lodges in America in 1973 and 1976, they all say the same thing: "If you want to worship Christ, go to your church; we worship the Grand Architect of the Universe (the god of the Freemasons) here."

Penalties Enforced

Freemasonry has been accused of carrying out promises to murder those who would reveal their secrets, and the evidence of those accusations is overwhelming.

Captain William Morgan is a significant figure to consider as far as these penalties are concerned. After his murder, it is estimated that forty-five thousand Masons quit Masonic lodges, leaving probably less than ten thousand. More than two thousand lodges were disbanded. Albert Mackey had this to say about Morgan in his book, *Encyclopedia of Freemasonry* (page 508):

> Morgan, William, born in 1775. He published in 1826 a pretended Exposition of Masonry, which attracted more attention than it deserved. Morgan soon after disappeared, and the Masons were charged by some enemies of the order with having removed him by foul means. The real fate of Morgan has never been ascertained. There are various myths of his disappearance and subsequent residence in other countries. These may or may not be true, but it is certain that there is no evidence of his death which has been admitted in court or Probate.
>
> He was a man of questionable character and dissolute habit, and his enmity to Masonry is said to have originated from the refusal of the Masons of LeRay to admit him to membership in their lodge and chapter.

Mackey stated that Morgan's book was a pretended exposition of Masonry. I have read Morgan's book. It is *not* a pretended exposition. It is, in fact, a true exposition of the actual ritual of Freemasonry.

Rev. Charles Finney, who was a Mason and renounced it, in his book entitled *The Character, Claims, and Practical Workings of Freemasonry*, made the following statement in regard to Captain Morgan in 1879 (pp. 78-79), "At the time of the murder of Morgan, it was found that to such an extent were these offices in the hands of Freemasons, that the courts were entirely impotent."

The following is a quote from Mr. Stearn's letters on Freemasonry (p. 127):

> In speaking of the murder of William Morgan, of the justice of it, and of the impossibility of punishing his murderers, a justice of the peace in Middlebury, a sober, respectable man and a Mason, said that a man had a right to pledge his life and then observed, "Who are your judges? What can a rat do with a lion? Who are your sheriffs? And who will be your jurymen?"

Rev. Finney stated,

> It is perfectly plain that if Freemasons mean anything by this oath, as they have given frequent evidence that they do, this obligation must be an effectual bar to the administration of justice where Freemasons are numerous. No wonder, therefore, that dishonest men among them are very anxious greatly to multiply their numbers. In the days of William Morgan, they had so multiplied their number that it was found impossible, and in these days Freemasons have become so numerous, that in many places, it will be found impossible to execute the criminal law.

Following is a detailed description of the kidnapping and execution of Captain William Morgan as recorded in Rev. Charles Finney's book, *The Character, Claims, and Practical Workings of Freemasonry*, written in 1879, copyrighted, sold, and transferred to Ezra A. Cook and Co. in Chicago, Illinois, on March 14, 1879.

This book is available in the Library of Congress in Washington, D.C. Many Masons do not know the facts behind this case or where the documented facts can be obtained. Hence, the necessary information is given here so that the reader may look it up for himself. Also, a lengthy quote is required for the reader to get the full impact of the satanic origin and practices of Freemasonry as seen from the eyes of a great man of God who was thirty-four years old when these events took place. He was an eyewitness, not to the murder, but to all the evidences pro and con that followed. This is the exact quote from Rev. Finney's book:

> A publisher by the name of Miller, also residing in Batavia, agreed to publish what Mr. Morgan would write. This, coming to be known to Freemasons, led them to conspire for his destruction. This, as we shall see, was only in accordance with their oaths. By their oaths they were bound to seek his destruction, and to execute upon him the penalty of these oaths.
>
> They kidnapped Morgan and for a time concealed him in the magazine of the United States Fort—Fort Niagara, at the mouth of the Niagara River, where it empties into Lake Ontario. They kept him there until they could arrange to dispatch him. In the meantime, the greatest efforts were made to discover his whereabouts, and what the Masons had done with him. Strong suspicions

came finally to be entertained that he was confined
to that fort; and the Masons, finding that those sus-
picions were abroad, hastened his death. Two or
three have since, upon their deathbed, confessed
their part in the transaction. They drowned him in
the Niagara River. The account of the manner in
which this was done will be found in a book published by Elder Stearns, a Baptist elder. The book
is entitled *Stearns on Masonry*. It contains the deathbed confession of one of the murderers of William
Morgan. On page 311 of that work, you will find
that confession. But as many of my readers have not
access to that work, I take the liberty to quote it
entire, as follows:

"CONFESSION.

"The murder of William Morgan, confessed by
the man who, with his own hands, pushed him out
of the boat into Niagara River!

"The following account of that tragical scene is
taken from a pamphlet entitled 'Confession of the
murder of William Morgan, as taken down by Dr.
John L. Emery, of Racine County Wisconsin, in the
summer of 1848, and now (1849) first given to the
public.'

"This confession was taken down as related
by Henry L. Valance, who acknowledges himself
to have been one of the three who were selected
to make a final disposition of the ill-fated victim
of Masonic vengeance. This confession it seems
was made to his physicians, and in view of his

approaching dissolution, and published after his decease.

"After committing that horrid deed he was, as might well be expected, an unhappy man by day and by night. He was much like a Cain—'a fugitive and a vagabond.' To use his own words, 'Go where I would, or do what I would, it was impossible for me to throw off the consciousness of crime. If the mark of Cain was not upon me, the curse of the first murderer was—the bloodstain was upon my hands and could not be washed out.'

"He therefore commences his confession thus: 'My last hour is approaching; and as the things of this world fade from my mental sight, I feel the necessity of making, as far as in my power lies, that atonement which every violator of the great law of right owes to his fellowmen.' In this violation of the law, he says, 'I allude to the abduction and murder of the ill-fated William Morgan.'

"He proceeds with an interesting narrative of the proceedings of the fraternity in reference to Morgan, while he was incarcerated in the magazine of Fort Niagara. I have room for a few extracts only, showing the final disposition of their alleged criminal. Many consultations were held, 'many plans proposed and discussed, and rejected.' At length being driven to the necessity of doing something immediately for fear of being exposed, it was resolved in a council of eight, that he must die; must be consigned to a 'confinement from which there is no possibility of escape—THE GRAVE.' Three of their number were to be selected by ballot to execute the deed. Eight pieces of paper were procured, five of which were to remain blank, while the letter *D* was written on the others. These pieces of paper were placed in a large box, from which each man was to draw one at the same moment. 'After drawing we were all to separate, without looking at the paper that each held in his hand. So soon as we had arrived at certain distances from the place of rendezvous, the tickets were to be examined, and those who held blanks were to return instantly to their homes; and those who should hold marked tickets were to proceed to the fort at midnight, and there put Morgan to death, in such a manner as should seem to themselves most fitting.' Mr. Valance was one of the three who drew the ballots on which was the signal letter. He returned to the fort, where he was joined by his two companions, who had drawn the death tickets. Arrangements were made immediately for executing the sentence passed upon their prisoner, which was to sink him in the river with weights; in hope, says Mr. Valance, 'that he and our crime alike would thus be buried beneath the waves.' His part was to proceed to the magazine where Morgan was confined, and announce to him his fate; theirs was to procure a boat and weights with which to sink him. Morgan, on being informed of their proceedings against him, demanded by what authority they had condemned him, and who were his judges. 'He commenced wringing his hands, and talking of his wife and children, the recollections of whom, in that awful hour, terribly affected

147

him. His wife, he said, was young and inexperienced, and his children were but infants; what would become of them were he cut off, and they even ignorant of his fate?' What husband and father would not be 'terribly affected' under such circumstances—to be cut off from among the living in this inhuman manner?

"Mr. V.'s comrades returned, and informed him that they had procured the boat and weights, and that all things were in readiness on their part. Morgan was told that all his remonstrances were idle, that die he must, and that soon, even before the morning light. The feelings of the husband and father were still strong within him, and he continued to plead on behalf of his family. They gave him one half hour to prepare for his 'inevitable fate.' They retired from the magazine and left him. 'How Morgan passed that time,' says Mr. Valance, 'I cannot tell, but everything was quiet as the tomb within.' At the expiration of the allotted time, they entered the magazine, laid hold of their victim, 'bound his hands behind him, and placed a gag in his mouth.' They then led him forth to execution. 'A short time,' says this murderer, 'brought us to the boat, and we all entered it—Morgan being placed in the bow with myself alongside of him. My comrades took the oars, and the boat was rapidly forced out into the river. The night was pitch dark, we could scarcely see a yard before us, and therefore was the time admirably adapted to our hellish purpose.' Having reached a proper distance from the shore, the oarsmen ceased their labors. The weights were all secured together by a strong cord, and another cord of equal strength, and of several yards in length, proceeded from that. 'This cord,' says Mr. V., 'I took in my hand (did not that hand tremble?) and fastened it around the body of Morgan, just above his hips, using all my skill to make it fast, so that it would hold. Then, in a whisper, I bade the unhappy man to stand up, and after a momentary hesitation he complied with my order. He stood close to the head of the boat, and there was just length enough of rope from his person to the weights to prevent any strain, while he was standing. I then requested one of my associates to assist me in lifting the weights from the bottom to the side of the boat, while the others steadied her from the stern. This was done, and, as Morgan was standing with back toward me, I approached him and gave him a strong push with both my hands, which were placed on the middle of his back. He fell forward, carrying the weights with him, and the waters closed over the mass. We remained quiet for two or three minutes, when my companions, without saying a word, resumed their places, and rowed the boat to the place from which they had taken it.'"

They also kidnapped Mr. Miller, the publisher; but the citizens of Batavia, finding it out, pursued the kidnappers, and finally rescued him.

The courts of justice found themselves entirely unable to make any headway against the widespread conspiracy that was formed among Masons in respect to this matter.

These are matters of record. It was found that they could do nothing with the courts, with the sheriffs, with the witnesses, or with the jurors; and all their efforts were for a time entirely impotent. Indeed, they never were able to prove the murder of Morgan, and bring it home to the individuals who perpetrated it.

But Mr. Morgan had published Freemasonry to the world. The greatest pains were taken by Masons to cover up the transaction, and as far as possible to deceive the public in regard to the fact that Mr. Morgan had published Masonry as it really is.

Masons themselves, as is affirmed by the very best authority, published two spurious editions of Morgan's book, and circulated them as the true edition which Morgan had published. These editions were designed to deceive Masons who had never seen Morgan's edition, and thus to enable them to say that it was not a true revelation of Masonry.

In consequence of the publication of Morgan's book, and the revelations that were made in regard to the kidnapping and murdering of Mr. Morgan, great numbers of Masons were led to consider the subject more fully than they had done; and the conscientious among them almost universally renounced Masonry altogether. I believe that about two thousand lodges, as a consequence of these revelations, were suspended.

The ex-president of a Western college, who is himself a Freemason, has recently published some very important information on the subject, though he justifies Masonry. He says that, out of a little more than fifty thousand Masons in the United States at that time, forty-five thousand turned their backs upon the lodge to enter the lodge no more. Conventions were called of Masons that were disposed to renounce it. One was held at Leroy, another at Philadelphia, and others at other places. I do not now remember where. The men composing these conventions made public confession of their relation to the institution, and publicly renounced it. At one of these large conventions they appointed a committee to superintend the publication of Masonry in all its degrees. This committee was composed of men of first-rate character, and men quite generally known to the public. Elder Bernard, a Baptist elder in good standing, was one of this committee; and he, with the assistance of his brethren who had been appointed to this work, obtained an accurate version of some forty-eight degrees. He published also the proceedings of those conventions, and much concerning the efforts that were made by the courts to search the matter to the bottom; and also several speeches that were made by prominent men in the state of New York. This work was entitled *Light on Masonry*. In this work any person who is disposed may get a very correct view of what Freemasonry really is. This and sundry other reliable works on Freemasonry may be had at Godrich's and Fitch & Fairchild's bookstores, in Oberlin. In saying this, it is proper to add that I have no direct or indirect pecuniary interest in the sale of those or of any book on Freemasonry whatever, nor shall I have in the sale of this which I am now preparing for the press. Freemasons shall not with truth accuse me of self-interest in exposing their institutions.

Before the publication of Bernard's *Light on Masonry*, great pains were taken to secure the most accurate knowledge of the degrees published by the committee, as the reader of that work will see, if he reads the book through. An account of all these matters will be found in *Light on Masonry*, to which I have referred. In the Northern or non-slave holding States, Masonry was almost universally renounced at that time. But it was found that it had taken so deep a root that in all New England there was scarcely a newspaper in which the death of William Morgan, and the circumstances connected therewith, could be published. This was generally true throughout all the North that newspapers had to be everywhere established for the purpose of making the disclosures that were necessary in regard to its true character and tendency. The same game is being played over again at the present day. The *Cynosure*, the new anti-Mason paper published at Chicago, is constantly intercepted on its way to subscribers. Four of its first six numbers failed to reach me, and now in December 1868, I have received no number later than the sixth. The editor informs me that the numbers are constantly intercepted. The public will be forced to learn what a lawless and hideous institution Freemasonry is.

It was found that Masonry so completely baffled the courts of law, and obstructed the course of justice, that it was forced into politics; and for a time the anti-Masonic sentiment of the Northern States carried all before it. Almost all Masons became ashamed of it, felt themselves disgraced by having any connection with it, and publicly renounced it. If they did not publish any renunciation, they suspended their lodges, had no more to do with it, and did not pretend to deny that Masonry had been published.

Now these facts were so notorious, so universally known and confessed, that those of us who were acquainted with them at the time had no idea that Masonry would have the impudence, ever again to claim any public respect. I should just as soon expect slavery to be reestablished in this country, and become more popular than ever before—to take possession of the Government and of all civil offices, and to grow bold, impudent, and defiant—as I should have expected that Masonry would achieve what it has. When the subject of Freemasonry was first forced upon our churches in Oberlin, for discussion and action, I cannot express the astonishment, grief, and indignation that I felt upon hearing professed Christian Freemasons deny either expressly or by irresistible implication that Morgan and others had truly revealed the secrets of Freemasonry. But a few years ago such denial would have ruined the character of any intelligent man, not to say of a professed Christian.

But I must say, also, that Masonry itself had its literature. Many bombastic and spread-eagle books have been published in its favor. They never attempt to justify it as it is revealed in *Light on Masonry*, nor reply by argument to the attacks that have been so successfully made upon it; neither have they pretended to reveal its secrets. But they have eulogized it in a manner that is utterly nauseating to those that understood what it really is. But these books have been circulated among the young, and have no doubt led thousands of scores of thousands of young men into the Masonic ranks, who, but for these miserable productions, would never have thought of taking such a step.

Rev. Finney made this statement in one of his other books:

I wish, if possible, to arouse the young men who are Freemasons and Christians to consider the inevitable consequences of such a horrible trifling with the most solemn oaths, as is constantly practiced by Freemasons. Such a course must and does, as a matter of fact, grieve the Holy Spirit, sear the conscience, and harden the heart.

John Quincy Adams, who was president of the United States from 1825 until 1829, spoke out against Masonry, as well:

Because of the excitement produced by the murder of Morgan; of the facts that were brought to light by the testimony of witness before the court; of the action of the New York Legislature; and of the defense of Masonry by the Grand Lodge of Rhode Island, the scholarly John Quincy Adams was led to make an impartial examination and investigation of Masonry. He did so from purely patriotic motives. We give his views as they are expressed in letters and in his address to the people of Massachusetts. He says, "I saw a code of Masonic legislature adapted to prostrate every principle of equal justice and to corrupt every sentiment of virtuous feeling in the soul of him who bound his allegiance to it. I saw the practice of common honesty, the kindness of Christians benevolence, even the abstinence of atrocious crimes, limited exclusively by lawless oaths and barbarous penalties, to the social relations between the brotherhood and the craft. I saw slander organize into a secret, widespread, and affiliated agency, fixing its invisible fangs into the hearts of its victims, sheltered by the darkness of the lodge room and armed with the never-ceasing penalties of death. I saw self-invoked imprecation of throats cut from ear to ear, of hearts and vitals torn out and cast off and hung on spires. I saw wine drank from a human skull with solemn invocation of all the sins of its owner upon the head of him who drank it. I saw a wretched mortal man dooming himself to eternal punishment when the last trump shall sound, as a guarantee for idle and ridiculous promises. Such are the laws of Masonry, such are their indelible character, and with that character perfectly corresponds the history of Masonic lodges, chapters, encampments, and consistories, from that day to the present. A conspiracy of the few against the equal rights of the many; anti-republican in its sap, from the first blushing of the summit of the plant, to the deepest fiber of its root. Notwithstanding these horrid oaths and penalties of which a common cannibal would be ashamed, the general Grand Royal Arch Chapter of the U.S.A. forbade their abandonment. That Masonry sanctions these barbarities is therefore proven beyond a question."[2]

That statement, after careful investigation into the order was made by the president of the United States in 1826 (serving when Morgan was murdered), came about to be recorded by M. L. Wagner.

The twenty-fifth landmark of Freemasonry states in brief that all of the landmarks of Freemasonry cannot be changed. Nothing can be subtracted from them—nothing can be added to them, not the slightest modification can be made in them! Not one iota of these unwritten laws can be repealed. If nothing in their rituals and oaths can be changed, what can be said for today? Can Freemasonry claim, "Well, that was many years ago, we are not evil or sinful like our misguided brothers." God's Word says in 2 Timothy 3:1-5,

This know, also, that in the last days perilous times shall come. For men shall be lovers of their own selves, covetous, boasters, proud, blasphemers, disobedient to parents, unthankful, unholy, without natural affection, trucebreakers, false accusers, incontinent, fierce, despisers of those that are good, traitors, heady, high-minded, lovers of pleasures more than lovers of God, having a form of godliness, but denying the power of it; from such turn away.

These verses in 2 Timothy 3 describe what President Adams and Rev. Finney have said about Freemasonry. God's Word says *"from such turn away."* Verse thirteen of this same chapter says, *"But evil men and seducers shall wax worse and worse, deceiving, and being deceived."* God said that in the last days men will go from bad to worse. What happened to William Morgan so many years ago was bad; God says that it is worse today. Man's sinfulness and ability to do what was done to Morgan is as great today as in 1826.

---

[1]Rev. John R. Rice, *Lodges Examined by the Bible* (Murfreesboro, TN: Sword of the Lord Foundation, 1931).

[2]Martin L. Wagner, *Freemasonry: An Interpretation* (Chicago: Ezra A. Cook), 164.

Ten

Points of Interest

❖

Masonic Bible Beliefs

In this chapter, some of the quotations in Masonic Bibles will be covered and compared with God's Word.

"The Holy Bible is the great light in Masonry and the rule and guide for faith and practice." As has been proved by the pagan rituals and blood-curdling oaths, Masonry most assuredly makes a mockery of God in claiming the Bible as its guide for faith and practice. Masonry's practices are anti-Christian. It is a work-oriented cult, and faith has nothing to do with its teaching. The word *faith* is never used in a biblical sense. Freemasonry accepts Hindus and Muslims. To the Muslim, the Koran is his Bible, and he uses it for the rule and guide of his faith. To the Hindu, the Vedas is used as his rule and guide. When Freemasonry speaks of the Bible, it is not speaking of the New Testament theology in light of Jesus Christ. Masonry's definition of holy writ depends on which religion is being discussed. Many Christian Masons believe they are worshipping God in the lodge room because of clever manipulations of biblical terminology, but, in fact, they are honoring the god of Masonry. This god is the god of naturalism, not the Bible's God as revealed in Christ.

A statement made by Rev. Joseph Fort Newton in the Masonic Bible follows. (The title over Rev. Newton's name is *The Words of a Great Masonic Divine*):

> And yet, like everything else in Masonry, the Bible, so rich in symbolism, is itself a symbol that is a part taken from the whole. It is a sovereign symbol of the Book of Faith, the will of God as man has learned it in the midst of the years—that perpetual revelation of himself which God is making mankind in every land and every age. Thus, by the very honor which Masonry pays to the Bible, it teaches us to revere every book of faith in which men find help for today and hope for tomorrow, joining hands with the man of Islam as he takes oath on the Koran, and the Hindu as he makes covenant with God upon the book he loves best.

Rev. Newton used the word *faith* in his statement, yet his statement clearly mocks the biblical definition of faith.

"Man is immortal." This is a true statement. What is untrue is the explanation given to Masons regarding the immortality of man. Masonry's teachings on eternal life are never Christ-centered. Freemasonry spends all its degree work trying to improve man's character, and it is character building, as it is called, that "leads a man to his destiny, that house not made with hands."

John 10:9-10 reads,

> *I am the door: by me if any man enter in, he shall be saved, and shall go in and out, and find pasture. The thief cometh not, but to steal, and to kill, and to destroy: I am come that they might have life, and that they might have it more abundantly.*

Jesus is the door to abundant life, not human character that has been improved by one's own effort.

Fatherhood of God, Brotherhood of Man

All Masonic Bibles attempt to explain the Fatherhood of God and Brotherhood of Man. In backing up their position on the Fatherhood of God, most authors quote Scripture dealing with creation. God is the Creator of all things; this is clearly indicated in Scripture. But He is not the Father of all mankind. Why Freemasonry quotes creation passages and then speaks of Fatherhood does not make sense. He created the animals, too, but He is not their Father; He is their Creator. Fatherhood indicates relationship or fellowship; the term *Creator* does not. First Corinthians 1:9 says, *"God is faithful, by whom ye were called unto the fellowship of his Son Jesus Christ our Lord."* First John 1:3 says, *"That which we have seen and heard declare we unto you, that ye also may have fellowship with us: and truly our fellowship is with the Father, and with his Son Jesus Christ."* Second John 9 says, *"Whosoever transgresseth, and abideth not in the doctrine of Christ, hath* not God. *He that abideth in the doctrine of Christ, he hath both the Father and the Son.*" These verses show the true meaning of Fatherhood as it is found in the fellowship of a relationship with God.

Freemasonry believes that since God is the Creator of mankind, He is also the Father of all mankind. It is clear that the only way Freemasonry could bring all religions together is to project a Fatherhood of God doctrine. Once it is established that God becomes the Father of all mankind, it is not hard to conceive how Freemasonry spreads the heresy of the Brotherhood of Mankind. Romans 8:8–10 says,

> *So then they that are in the flesh cannot please God. But ye are not in the flesh but in the Spirit, if so be that the Spirit of God dwell in you. Now if any man have not the Spirit of Christ, he is none of his. And if Christ be in you, the body is dead because of sin, but the Spirit is life because of righteousness.*

Romans 8:14–16 says,

> *For as many as are led by the Spirit of God, they are the sons of God. For ye have not received the spirit of bondage again to fear; but ye have received the Spirit of adoption, whereby we cry, Abba, Father. The Spirit himself beareth witness with our spirit, that we are the children of God.*

Tracts put out by the various Grand Lodges in the United States also support the teachings of Masonry found in their Masonic Bibles. Here is a quote taken from a tract put out by the Grand Lodge of the state of Maryland. The title of the tract is "Freemasonry—A Way of Life." Under the paragraph entitled, "What is Freemasonry?" it reads as follows:

> Freemasonry is not an insurance or beneficial society. It is not organized for profits. However, the charity and services rendered are beyond measure. It teaches monotheism. It teaches the Golden Rule. It seeks to make good men better through its firm belief in the Fatherhood of God, the Brotherhood of Man, and the Immortality of the Soul.

Freemasonry firmly believes in the Fatherhood of God and the Brotherhood of Man. It also claims to teach monotheism which, at first glance, would ensnare some Christians, knowing that Christianity is also monotheistic. But the difference is that Freemasonry is Unitarian in doctrine, not Trinitarian, as Christianity is. Christians believe in one God, but only as revealed in three persons, the Father, Son, and Holy Spirit. Freemasonry does not teach or believe this. All the Masonic rituals and writings of great Masonic authors make this point very clear. Also, if Freemasonry were Trinitarian, there would be only Christians in lodges, which is certainly not true. Freemasonry embraces religion and sacred writings from all over the world.

Some Grand Lodges claim to be only religious, not promoters of a religion. But that claim would be contrary to teaching the Golden Rule, Fatherhood of God, Brotherhood of Man, eternal life, using the Bible, its verses and terminology, kneeling at altars, having prayers, having priests and chaplains—all elements of a religion.

In considering what someone else has to say about Freemasonry's claims of Fatherhood of God and Brotherhood of Man, the following is from *Christ or the Lodge*, put out by Great Commission Publications in Philadelphia, Pennsylvania (pp. 20-21):

> Scripture tells us that God made of one blood every nation of men to dwell on all the face of the earth (Acts 17:26). Therefore, it's not amiss to assert that there is a physical brotherhood of all men. It may even be admitted that by virtue of such remnants in fallen man, of the original image of God as reason and conscience, all men are brothers in more than a physical sense.

But Scripture emphatically denies that the universal brotherhood of man is spiritual. On the contrary, it teaches that there is an absolute spiritual antithesis between believers and unbelievers. Spiritually, they are opposites, like righteousness and iniquity, light and darkness, Christ and Belial (2 Corinthians 6:14-15). Masonry boasts of the brotherhood of its members and glories in the universal Brotherhood of Man. J. F. Newton said, "If one were asked to define Masonry in a single sentence, it would be to say, 'Masonry is the realization of God by the practice of brotherhood.'" He went on to describe universal brotherhood as physical, intellectual, and spiritual. It is spiritual, he believed, because while religions are many, religion is one. He added that the genius of the religion of Jesus was the extension of the idea of the family to include all humanity.[1]

E. A. Coil said,

> It is becoming more and more clear to me as the facts relating to the subject are brought out that the fraternity and churches called liberal have been working along parallel lines; but, because the one puts the chief emphasis upon the Fatherhood of God, and therefore emphasizes theology, while the other puts the chief emphasis upon the brotherhood of man, and therefore emphasizes sociology, they have realized that they were occupying practically the same ground.[2]

There are Grand Lodges and subordinate lodges in every state spreading this counterfeit gospel. They are linked with approximately a hundred other Grand Lodges in countries all over the world. All teach the same basic Masonic tenets. All members are bound together by the oaths, regardless of their religious beliefs, as long as they believe in a Supreme Being and the immortality of the soul.

Masonic Funeral Services

Turning to another aspect of Freemasonry, a black book is used for funeral services or memorial services usually performed at the funeral home, church, or graveside. In the front of this black book is a paragraph that is a standing resolution: "A lodge can bury a brother Master Mason only when requested to do so by him or his family and provided he was affiliated and in good standing at the time of his death."

Should a lodge be called upon to bury a brother, it must have exclusive control of the funeral; all pallbearers must be Masons, and the funeral service of the lodge must be conducted immediately after the service of the church.

The lodge members may attend the funeral, even though other societies attend, but it cannot allow any other society to participate in the ceremonies, until the Masonic ceremonies are fully completed.

Who actually has the last rites over a deceased Christian who is a Mason? It is the lodge, not the church, and Masonry must be in exclusive control of the funeral. The Worshipful Master of the lodge gives the same speech at the memorial service of a deceased Mason whether he is Christian or Jew. There are officers and lodge members present to conduct this service wearing pagan jewels and aprons, white gloves and a high hat. They are lined in a semi-circle next to the casket, facing the family and friends present.

The Master of the lodge begins,

> Masonry has come down from the far past. It uses the tools of the builder's trade as emblems and symbols to teach Masons how to build character and moral stature. It teaches service to God, to a brother, and to all mankind. It seeks constantly to build the temple of the soul and thus fit us for that house not made with hands, eternal in the heavens. Masonry

is a fellowship that unites Masons in friendship and goodwill. It teaches the spiritual values of life that lie beyond the physical senses. Masonry confronts the fact of death with the greater fact of faith in the immortality of the soul. Masons believe in the immortality of the soul. Masons believe sincerely that when life on earth comes to a close, the soul is translated from the imperfections of this mortal sphere, to that all perfect, glorious, and celestial lodge above, where God, the Grand Architect of the Universe, presides.

With these truths and convictions our brother was well acquainted. Though perfection of character is not of this world, yet we are persuaded that our brother sought to live by these truths and principles of Masonry; that they sustained and supported him; and that by them his life was made richer, fuller, and more meaningful.

When our brother labored with us in Masonic attire, he wore a white apron, which he was taught is an emblem of innocence and the badge of a Mason. By it he was constantly reminded of that purity of life, and that rectitude of conduct, so necessary to his gaining admission into the celestial lodge above. He will now wear that apron forever as the emblem of our faith in the immortality of the soul. By it, we are reminded of the immortality of the soul which survives the grave, and which will never, never die.

The belief that good works, represented by the apron, will gain admission into heaven, comes straight from the evil one. Ephesians 2:8-9 says, *"For by grace are ye saved through faith; and that not of yourselves: it is the gift of God: not of works, lest any man should boast."*

[1] *The Religion of Masonry*, 116–123.

[2] *The Relationship of the Liberal Churches and the Fraternal Orders*, 9–10.

Eleven

Ceremony of Installation of a Worshipful Master

❧

T he Worshipful Master presides over the foundational, or first three, degrees of all Masonry. It is
here that the roots of the beliefs and dogma are to
be found. All other degrees are grafted branches into the
heart of the tree of the Blue Lodge.

All the points of the installation ceremonies of the
officers cannot be covered here because of limited space.
A couple of points of the ceremonies involving the
Worshipful Master, the highest officer in the Blue Lodge,
will be covered. There are fifteen questions that are asked
of the Worshipful Master being installed. The first point
he must assent to is, "You agree to be a good man and
true, and strictly obey the Moral Law."

The only way anyone is to be good and true in God's
sight is to be in Christ. It is the righteousness of Christ
that God sees when He looks at a Christian. It is through
the presence of the indwelling Holy Spirit that Christians
are empowered to be good and true men.

This first statement also charges the Worshipful Master to strictly obey the Moral Law. The Bible says in Romans 3:19-24,

> Now we know that what things soever the law saith, it saith to them who are under the law: that every mouth may be stopped, and all the world may become guilty before God. Therefore, by the deeds of the law there shall no flesh be justified in his sight: for by the law is the knowledge of sin. But now the righteousness of God without the law is manifested, being witnessed by the law and the prophets; even the righteousness of God which is by faith of Jesus Christ unto all and upon all them that believe: for there is no difference: for all have sinned, and come short of the glory of God; being justified freely by his grace through the redemption that is in Christ Jesus.

Scripture says in Galatians 2:16-21,

> Knowing that a man is not justified by the works of the law, but by the faith of Jesus Christ, even we have believed in Jesus Christ, that we might be justified by the faith of Christ, and not by the works of the law: for by the works of the law shall no flesh be justified. But if, while we seek to be justified by Christ, we ourselves also are found sinners, is therefore Christ the minister of sin? God forbid. For if I build again the things which I destroyed, I make myself a transgressor. For I through the law am dead to the law, that I might live unto God. I am crucified with Christ: nevertheless I live; yet not I, but Christ liveth in me: and the life which I now live in the flesh I live by the faith of the Son of God, who loved me, and gave himself for me. I do not frustrate the

grace of God: for if righteousness come by the law, then Christ is dead in vain.

Galatians 3:24 says, "*Wherefore the law was our school-master to bring us unto Christ, that we might be justified by faith.*" The perfect righteousness of Christ has already been obtained for us at Calvary. A Christian being installed as a Worshipful Master promises to keep the Moral Law strictly, yet he is frustrating the grace of God and living by sight and works, not by faith in the shed blood of Christ.

Point number five in these charges is this:

> You agree to hold in veneration the original rules and patrons of Masonry and their regular successors, supreme and subordinate, according to their stations; and to submit to the awards and resolutions of your brethren when convened, in every case consistent with the constitution of the Grand Lodge.

A Mason is to give his assent to submit to the awards and resolutions of the members of his lodge. Is it possible for a Christian to submit to the resolutions of the members and yet be submitted to Christ?

The next point of concern is number eight, which reads, "You promise to respect genuine brethren, and to discountenance imposters and all dissenters from the original plan of Masonry." Who are genuine brethren? According to Freemasonry, a brother is one who has been accepted and initiated into the degrees of Freemasonry and will adhere to its teachings. God's definition of genuine brethren is found in Matthew 12:48–50, where Jesus said,

> But he answered and said unto him that told him, Who is my mother? and who are my brethren? And he stretched forth his hand toward his disciples, and said, Behold my mother and my brethren! For whosoever shall do the will of my Father which is in heaven, the same is my brother, and sister, and mother.

What is the will of the Father? John 6:40 states,

> And this is the will of him that sent me, that every one which seeth the Son, and believeth on him, may have everlasting life: and I will raise him up at the last day.

Next, the Mason is to "discountenance imposters and all dissenters from the original plan of Masonry." What is the original plan of Masonry? One way to summarize this briefly is to state what Freemasonry's original plan is not. It is not to make men conformable to the person of Jesus Christ. Masonry's plan is not to have men obedient to the Word of God. It is not their original plan to have men walk by faith or confess Jesus Christ as Savior and Redeemer of all mankind.

Everything that is counter and opposite to the Word of God, especially as revealed by the person of Christ, is what Freemasonry's original plan is for their members. It seeks to mold them into its misinterpretations of who and what God is, and His plan for them in a well-spent life, leading all by false teachings to hell.

Points Nine and Ten of
Installation of Worshipful Master

Point number nine is this: "You agree to promote the general good of society, to cultivate the social virtues, and to propagate the knowledge of the art." First, we see that this new Master is to agree to promote the general good of society. To do this, he must have some plan in mind. Since we know that Freemasonry's plan is not laid on the foundation of Christ, it could be concluded that it is anti-Christian and contrary to God's Word.

All of Masonry's teachings are devoid of a personal, biblical interpretation of Jesus Christ. The need to be born again; the doctrine of the deity of Christ; the blood atonement; and a belief in the inerrant, absolute, inspired Word of God are not part of Masonic teachings, yet there are doctrinal teachings in all of these areas.

To promote the general good of society, one would have to preach and teach Jesus Christ and His saving grace, and live a life well-pleasing to Him in obedience to His written Word. Masonry's interpretation of the general good of society means to promote and lift up the teachings of the cult of Freemasonry. Instead of promoting the real need of society, the Mason, using Masonic instruction, would be promoting a spiritually deprived society.

The Master must agree to cultivate the social virtues. Philippians 4:8–9 says,

> *Finally, brethren, whatsoever things are true, whatsoever things are honest, whatsoever things are just, whatsoever*

things are pure, whatsoever things are lovely, whatever
things are of good report; if there be any virtue, and if
there be any praise, think on these things. These things,
which ye have both learned, and received, and heard,
and seen in me, do: and the God of peace shall be with
you.

The Master is then told to propagate or spread forth the knowledge of the art of Freemasonry. The knowledge of the art of Freemasonry is to saturate men's minds with teachings that are religious, pious, ceremonial, ritualistic, but most importantly, completely and totally devoid of biblical truth.

Point number ten in the installation of the Master is this: "You promise to pay homage to the Grand Master for the time being and to his officers, when duly installed; and strictly conform to every edict of the Grand Lodge, or General Assembly of Masons, which is not subversive of the principle and groundwork of Masonry."

Homage includes reverence. We call ministers "Reverend." Can the same respect be given to the rulers and authorities in Masonry, who promote a counterfeit gospel?

A Mason is to conform to the edicts of the Grand Lodge that are not subversive, or ruinous, to the ground-work and principles of Masonry. Christianity is most assuredly subversive to the principles and groundwork of all the branches of Masonry. To be obedient to God's Word would place any Christian who is a Mason in a position that would be subversive to all of the principles of Masonry.

Twelve

New Horizons

O ne could say that "Once a Mason, always a
Mason" is the fixed result of the secrets to which
one has obligated himself in Masonry. However,
be reminded of what John 8:36 says: *"If the Son therefore
shall make you free, ye shall be free indeed."* The freedom
that Jesus gives is spiritual.

Masons who are not believers in the Lord Jesus
Christ will no doubt question the contents of this book.
An inability to discern real truth exists when the Spirit
of God does not indwell an individual. When a person
accepts the Lord Jesus Christ as his personal Savior, he
is filled with the Holy Spirit, who gives the ability to discern truth from error. Misunderstanding spiritual truth
can increase the difficulty of discerning those Masons
who are Christian from those who are not. Masons
who profess to be Christians are spiritually blind and
present a tremendous hindrance to the proclamation of
the Gospel of Jesus Christ.

Freemasonry is demonic in nature and presents a
tremendous spiritual obstacle to individual Christian

growth. For the person who has truly been redeemed by the shed blood of Jesus Christ, the lodge group can be extremely detrimental. It is for this reason that it should be avoided by Christians at all costs.

The foundational doctrines of the Christian faith proclaimed in the Bible provide the contrast with Freemasonry and associated teachings as a religious cult that borrows its doctrinal statements and practices from satan's worship laid in ancient times. Many men of God, such as Moody, Finney, Torrey, Barnhouse, and Rice, vigorously opposed Freemasonry. Some of these men had also been involved in Freemasonry at one time in their lives. God's Word is completely opposed to the teachings of Freemasonry.

If you are a Mason, but not a Christian, I urge you to consider your stand before almighty God. Confess your sinful condition, receive Christ as your personal Savior, and begin a new life in Christ. Put the past behind you and reach forward to a bright new future. Romans 6:23 says, *"For the wages of sin in death; but the gift of God is eternal life through Jesus Christ our Lord."* John 1:12 says, *"But as many as received him, to them gave he power to become the sons of God, even to them that believed on his name."* And 1 John 5:12 says, *"He that hath the Son hath life; and he that hath not the Son of God hath not life."*

If you are a Mason who loves the Lord Jesus Christ and wants to serve Him effectively as His child, please study the evidences again. Allow God's Word to be the judge and jury. Compare Christ's teachings with Freemasonry. You really can make only one choice.

For those who are Christians and not Masons, please meditate on the proofs offered in this book so that you will not be deceived into joining the lodge and thereby place yourself in a position of grieving God's Holy Spirit. Be faithful in witnessing for the Lord Jesus Christ, and do your part in preventing other believers from being entangled with this cult.

The signs of the times, compared with prophetic Scripture, make it apparent that we are living in the last days prior to the rapture of the church. Satan is hard at work trying to hinder believers' spiritual growth, as well as trying to keep the unsaved from entering God's family. Freemasonry is one of satan's master deceptions. Many ministers, elders, deacons, trustees, and Sunday school teachers belong to this cult. There is a tremendous need to scrutinize the cultic nature of Freemasonry in view of the massive infiltration of its effect on the working body of the church. It should be exposed to the true light—Jesus Christ.

Appendix

The following is the grip and word of an Entered Apprentice (first degree) and how it is received:

Worshipful Master: Brother, what is this?

Senior Warden: A grip.

WM: A grip of what?

SW: The grip of an Entered Apprentice.

WM: Has it a name?

SW: It has.

WM: Will you give it to me?

SW: I did not so receive it, neither can I so impart it.

WM: How will you dispose of it?

SW: I will letter it with you.

WM: Letter it and begin.

SW: Nay, you begin.

WM: Nay, begin you.

SW: A

WM: B

SW: O

WM: Z

SW: Bo

WM: az

The following is how Masons give the passgrip and word of a Fellowcraft (second degree Mason).

Worshipful Master: Brother, I hail.
Senior Warden: I conceal.
WM: What do you conceal?
SW: All the secrets of Masonry, except from him or them, to whom of right, the same belongs.
WM: Take me as I take you?

At this point, the Master takes the thumb of the brother and puts it on the first finger knuckle and does likewise with his own thumb. Then the Master says to the Senior Warden,

WM: What is this?
SW: A grip.
WM: A grip of what?
SW: The grip of an Entered Apprentice.
WM: Has it a name?
SW: It has.
WM: Will you give it to me?
SW: I did not to receive it, neither can I so impart it.
WM: How will you dispose of it?
SW: I will letter it with you.
WM: Letter it and begin.
SW: Nay, you begin.
WM: Nay, begin you.
SW: A
WM: B

SW: O
WM: Z
SW: Bo
WM: az

Then the Master puts the brother's thumb, as well as his, in the space between the first and second knuckle and says, "Pass on, what is this?"

SW: The passgrip of a Fellowcraft.
WM: Has it a name?
SW: It has.
WM: Will you give it to me?
SW: I did not so receive it, neither can I so impart it.
WM: How will you dispose of it?
SW: I will syllablic it with you.
WM: Syllablic it and begin.
SW: Nay, you begin.
WM: Nay, begin you.
SW: Shib
WM: bo
SW: leth

Then the Master looks at the brother at the altar and says, "Shibboleth, my brother, is the name of this grip, which is the passgrip of a Fellowcraft." The Master again moves both his and his brother's thumb to the second knuckle, on top of it, and says, "Pass on, what is this?"

SW: The grip of a Fellowcraft.
WM: Has it a name?
SW: It has.

WM: Will you give it to me?
SW: I did not so receive it, neither can I so impart it.
WM: How will you dispose of it?
SW: I will letter it with you.
WM: Letter it and begin.
SW: Nay, you begin.
WM: Nay, begin you.
SW: A
WM: J
SW: C
WM: H
SW: I
WM: N
SW: Ja
WM: chin

The Passgrip and Password of a Master Mason

Worshipful Master: Pass on, what is this? (The Master moves the brother's thumb as well as his own between the second and third knuckle.)
Senior Warden: The passgrip of a Master Mason.
WM: Has it a name?
SW: It has.
WM: Will you give it to me?
SW: I did not so receive it, neither can I so impart it.
WM: How will you dispose of it?
SW: I will syllablic it with you.
WM: Syllablic it and begin.

SW: Nay, you begin.
WM: Nay, begin you.
SW: Tu
WM: Bal
SW: Cain

Glossary

The following are the brief definitions of various words used throughout the book.

BLUE LODGES: Lodges used for the initiations of the first three degrees only. Also known as Craft Masonry.

DEGREES: The steps of progression through various initiations to which the candidate submits himself.

DUE GUARDS: Various movements of the arms, feet, and hands by the Mason, while in the lodge, to identify a mode assumed during his initiation. Each degree has its own due guard.

G.A.O.T.U.: Grand Architect of the Universe (the god of Masonry).

GRIPS: Handshakes used by Masons to identify the degree a brother may have obtained, as well as personal identification from one Mason to another.

HIRAM ABIFF: Master Architect on King Solomon's temple, brought to Jerusalem from Phoenicia by Hiram, king of Tyre (1 Kings 7).

LODGE (Operative): Guilds where the actual stone-masons meet for fellowship, which ceased in 1717.

LODGE (Speculative): The meeting place from 1717 to the present where candidates are initiated into the various degrees of Masonry.

MAH-HAH-BONE: In Hebrew it means "what this—the builder," referring to Hiram Abiff; also has pagan connotations from the ancient mysteries of the past.

SIGNS: Movements of usually the arms and hands in various ways to identify the death penalty a Mason is under in a particular degree. Every degree in Masonry has a sign.

Bibliography

Adams, John Quincy. *Speeches before Massachusetts Legislature, 1826.*

Akey, Denise S. *Encyclopedia of Associations.* 2 vols. Detroit: Gale Research Co., 1993.

Anderson, James. *Book of Constitutions of 1723.*

Buck, J. D. *Symbolism or Mystic Masonry.* Chicago: Ezra A. Cook, 1925.

Clausen, Henry C. *New Age Magazine.* Washington, D.C.: House of the Temple.

———. *What Is the Scottish Rite?* Washington, D.C.: House of the Temple, 1992.

Clymer, R. Swinburne. *The Mysticism of Masonry.* Philosophical Publishing Co., 1900.

Finney, Charles. *The Character, Claims, and Practical Workings of Freemasonry.* Chicago: Ezra A. Cook.

Hessey, John H., Bruce H. McDonald, and William F. Peitz. *Masonic Burial Service, Masonic Memorial Service.* Baltimore, MD: Harry S. Scott, 1960.

Johnson, David. *Dogs, Cats, and Communism.* Milton, FL: Gospel Projects, 1977.

Lady Queensborough. *Occult Theocracy.* Christian Book Club of America, 1931.

Lindsay, Hal. *The 1980s Countdown to Armageddon.* New York: Batah Books, 1980.

Mackey, Albert G. *Jurisprudence of Freemasonry.* 1872.

———. *Encyclopedia of Freemasonry.* Richmond, VA: Macoy Publishers and Masonic Supply Co., 1879.

———. *Manual of the Lodge.* New York: Clark and Maynard, 1970.

Maryland Manual of Ancient Craft Masonry. 1935.

Masonic Bible. Chicago: John A. Hertel Co.

Newton, Joseph F. *The Bible and Masonry.*

Orthodox Presbyterian Church. *Christ or the Lodge.* Philadelphia: Great Commission Publications, 1942.

Pierson. *Tradition of Freemasonry.*

Pike, Albert. *Morals and Dogma.* New York: H. Macoy, 1878.

Rice, John R. *Lodges Examined by the Bible.* Murfreesboro, TN: Sword of the Lord Foundation, 1931.

Spotlight Staff. *Spotlight Newspaper.* Washington, D.C.: 23 August 1980.

Stewart, Johnny. *Who Is Responsible?* Waco, TX: F.R.E.E.

Stewart, Thomas Milton. *Symbolic Teachings on Masonry and Its Message.* Cincinnati, Ohio: Stewart and Kidd, 1914.

Wagner, Martin L. *Freemasonry: An Interpretation.* Chicago: Ezra A. Cook.

Ward, J. S. *Freemasonry: Its Aims and Ideals.* Philadelphia: David McKay, 1925.

Webster, Nesta. *Secret Societies.* Christian Book Club of America, 1924.

ANOTHER POWERFUL BOOK

from Whitaker House

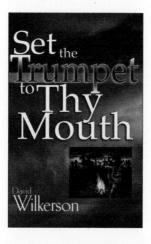

Set the Trumpet to Thy Mouth
David Wilkerson

Like the trumpet that warned ancient people of approaching dangers and armies, David Wilkerson calls attention to the insidious sins and compromises of our nation that may lead to the swift judgment of God. But he also brings a message of courage and comfort—a call to return to God with all our hearts and to fulfill God's purposes for us as His beloved children.

ISBN: 0-88368-640-6 Trade 224 pages

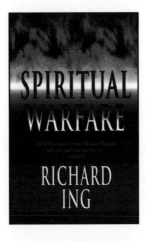